Learning
TO LEAD

Effective Leadership Skills
for Teachers of Young Children

Debra Ren-Etta Sullivan

Redleaf Press
St. Paul, Minnesota
www.redleafpress.org

PEARSON
Merrill
Prentice Hall

Upper Saddle River, New Jersey
Columbus, Ohio

This special edition is published by Merrill/Prentice Hall, by arrange-
ment with Redleaf Press, a divison of Resources for Child Caring, 450 N.
Syndicate, Suite 5, St. Paul, MN 55104.

Vice President and Executive Publisher: Jeffery W. Johnston
Acquisitions Editor: Julie Peters
Director of Marketing: Ann Castel Davis
Marketing Manager: Autumn Purdy
Marketing Coordinator: Brian Mounts

This book was printed and bound by Hamilton Printing Company. The
cover was printed by Phoenix Color Corp.

10 9 8 7 6 5 4 3 2 1
ISBN: 0-13-172790-7

To my husband, Scott,
and my children, Porter, Aaron, and Siobhan,
without whose love, patience, and support
this work would not have been possible

and in loving memory of Jocelyn Myres
whose love for children and all who teach them
served as powerful examples of the teacher
and the leader in each of us.

Acknowledgments

Many thanks to and much appreciation for my editor Beth Wallace and her ability to see what I really wanted to say. I give a very special thank you to my friends and colleagues at Pacific Oaks College Northwest and the Early Childhood Equity Alliance, who are listed below. Through our collaborative work and our ability to create one of the most multiracial, multilingual, multicultural teams I have ever experienced, I learned how to see the many faces of leadership and the many gifts we bring to the leadership process.

Veronica Barrera
Sharon Cronin
Fran Davidson
Louise Derman-Sparks
Wendy Harris
Cynthia Holloway
Theressa Lenear
Wei Li-Chen
Faye Louie
Mehret Mehanzel

Leticia Nieto
John Nimmo
Diana Puente
Merrilee Runyan
Joan Shelby
Tilman Smith
Zakiya Stewart
Susan Talaro
Lori Yonemitsu

Contents

Introduction

I have often been asked why I decided to write this book. There are numerous books out there on leadership, books for almost any field imaginable. For many years I have taught undergraduate and graduate leadership classes to students preparing for early childhood and elementary education. I have worked with preschool, kindergarten, and elementary teachers negotiating changes in student demographics, curriculum, building-level leadership, and staffing. I have presented conference workshops that bring together care providers, teachers, parents, and social service workers to create plans for collaboration that move away from what "others" should be doing and toward what each individual can do in the service, care, and education of children.

In all of these situations, I often come across the same two problems. First, many of the students in my classes see "true" leadership as something that belongs to "great" people, not something that they themselves are capable of. There is always a moment of surprise in class as students realized we are not going to talk about people like Martin Luther King, Mother Theresa, or Docia Zavitkovsky. Instead, the focus in my leadership classes is for students to examine their own roles in the leadership process.

Second, although the early childhood field continues to struggle with the challenges of a society that often overlooks the leadership potential, qualities, and abilities of those who care for and teach children, very little leadership literature is written for child care professionals who work directly with children. These are the people who share in the leadership process every day, spotting problems at whatever level they occupy and working toward solutions. These are the teachers, care providers, aides, and assistants who have direct responsibility for the care and education of young children.

While leadership applies to everyone connected with the field of early childhood care and education, this book focuses on the people who constitute the bulk of the early care and education field. They are people, such as you, who have always been and will continue to be part of the leadership process in many different environments and situations.

This book is about your personal development as a leader and as a teacher. If you work with children, you are a teacher. Even if you are just standing in a room with children you are a teacher. Children learn. That's all they do. It's their job. They learn from what you do and what you don't do. They learn from what you say and what you don't say. They learn from what you allow and what you won't allow. They learn from what you act on and what you don't act on. They learn from what you notice and what you don't notice. Children will learn from you how to treat people and what to expect of others. If children are present, they are learning. If you are present with them, you are teaching. (It is for this reason that the term "teacher" is used here to include all teachers, child care providers, aides, assistants, program/activity coordinators, and other staff, such as the cook, who work in early care and education settings.)

Leadership is similar. If you are interacting with other people, you are leading. How you behave with other people has an effect on what they think they can do, how they approach problems, and what they will consider. If other people are present, they are responding to you. They notice how you hold your body, whether you look tired or bored or interested or enthusiastic or angry. They hear how you react to questions, to problems, to changes, to good news. If you work in an organization like a child care center or a school, everything you do or don't do contributes to the way the organization functions. This is leadership.

Every adult needs to acknowledge, be responsible, and be accountable for the impact she has on the life of a child. Children look to us for learning and we are all providing those things whether we intend to or not. In the same way, you are leading whether you intend to or not, whether you are the director of the child care center, a home provider at a licensing meeting, or the infant room teacher. That's why it's so important to acknowledge your leadership—are you leading others in the direction you want to go?

Teaching and leading have other similarities. They involve many of the same skills. Because you are a good teacher, you can be a good leader as well. You are already doing it. You already know how. It's just a matter of recognizing your leadership and paying attention. You do this with children every day. You can do it with adults too.

This book is designed to give you an introduction to leadership theory and practice whether you work in a center, family child care, preschool, school-age care, or any other work environment involving children. You'll learn the definitions of what leadership is (and what it is not) and some functions and styles of leadership. You'll learn how to use your knowledge of child development to understand leadership development and how to transfer your leadership skills to a number of situations and circumstances. You'll learn about the roles of empowerment, followership, and advocacy in the leadership process as well as your own role in facilitating the leadership development of others.

Each chapter is built around a combination of theories, examples, and reflection questions—all designed so you have opportunities to fully examine and fully appreciate your own strengths, gifts, attitudes, values, challenges, and motivations, and how these influence your leadership development. And what good is a book if it doesn't contain some stories? Each chapter ends with a little vignette that puts some of the ideas you've read into action. It is not possible to include everything you need to know about leadership in one book, so I have also included ideas, information, and references for further practice, learning, and study.

Playing with blocks, children learn about weight, balance, gravity, construction, destruction, addition, subtraction, and how to work with other children. In much the same way that children transfer their play to learning possibilities, I hope you will transfer the knowledge you gain from reading this book to your everyday life. With this book, you will examine your ability to change the world. To the young child, all adults are leaders and have the power, authority, and status to change the world. Just turn the page to begin understanding and implementing what young children already know!

CHAPTER 1

Leadership in Early Childhood Education

In this chapter, I will discuss various ways of looking at leaders and leadership. You will have an opportunity to think about leadership's developmental nature, how the leadership process is mutually influenced by leaders and followers, and the many roles and words used to describe leaders. You will learn about the differences between leadership, power, authority, and status, and about the relationship between leadership development and human development. Finally, you will have an opportunity to think about what leadership means to you. But first, let's take a look at why we need leadership in our field and at the challenges and obstacles we face by the very nature of the fact that our profession is composed almost entirely of women working with children.

Why Do We Need Leaders and Leadership in Early Childhood Care and Education?

You and your three million colleagues serve approximately thirteen million children under the age of six, daily. Another three million children participate in after-school and summer programs and many millions more are in public or private primary grades. For each child, you and your colleagues serve as an important teacher. Each and every one of your words, actions, reactions, values, beliefs, interests, priorities, and perspectives (and a host of other things) will provide the children with a model of what kind of person they can become and what they should learn about their world. Such a big responsibility requires much leadership from many people. For the children in our classrooms, we look for teaching that is intellectually and creatively stimulating, developmentally and culturally appropriate for the children being served, and socially responsive to the needs of families and communities.

> We can be sure that if *we* are ambivalent about the need for and definition of leadership within our field, those on the outside looking in at us are even more confused.

Outside of the classroom, we look for curricular and organizational leadership from teachers. From directors and managers, we seek guidance and vision in staff training, the management of resources, setting goals and outcomes, and establishing good relationships with families and outside agencies. We seek political leadership in advocates who can give voice to issues such as worthy wages, clear and accessible career paths, and the impact of quality child care on the future of our children. From our neighborhoods and communities we hear the call for leaders in early care and education who address the needs and realities of families, form collaborative relationships for social change, and truly recognize the essential role of families and communities in raising children successfully.

The leadership through collaboration, cooperation, and communication on all our parts will improve and strengthen the whole system. Employees and advocates in the field may think of early childhood care and education (ECE) as a series of discrete environments and institutions serving children of a limited age range, but to children and families it is one continuous process that is all-connected and builds on previous experience. If leadership in ECE is to truly affect our children and families in beneficial ways, we must begin to view it from their perspectives. Viewing the educational system as a single entity can increase collaboration and cooperation between family child care, centers, school-age care, preschools, and elementary schools.

Over the course of your life, you may find yourself involved in many child-related contexts, as a parent or as a professional. For example, your work in community collaboration as a school-age care provider may become a critical part of your future as an advocate in a family services campaign. Your close and collaborative efforts with parents as a family child care provider may become the key ingredient of family involvement planning at a child care center. The firsthand experiences of children's developmental stages that you gain in your work at a child care center may influence your parenting style at home. And, in all of these, your ability to understand the impact of leadership on children and their families will help change society and the future of early childhood care and education in ways you can't begin to imagine!

Obstacles to Early Childhood Leadership

However, many obstacles get in the way of leadership in early childhood care and education. Our field is almost entirely composed of women who are drawn to a nurturing environment, working with young children, and participating in the growth of others, and who are willing to put the needs of others above their own. This makes it difficult to develop leaders, given that the leadership development process is self-focused, often rigorous or conflictual, and forces teachers to engage in situations and activities that may feel uncomfortable.

In addition, our field is often undervalued in society. The pay is low, the benefits are minimal or non-existent, the turnover is high, there are few entry requirements and even fewer opportunities for professional development or training, and the pathways for career advancement are unclear. We have yet to develop an inclusive definition of leadership that takes into account the leadership that is needed at all levels and in all areas. In many cases, people in early childhood are not even sure how they really feel about the concept of leadership. Because of this, they compete with each other (level against level, setting against setting, public against private) for the few resources that are available.

We can be sure that if we are ambivalent about the need for and definition of leadership within our field, those on the outside looking in at us are even more confused. Developing future leaders in such an environment is incredibly difficult! It has even been suggested that we are hesitant to provide too many rewards and incentives for leadership development because teachers with more skills may be drawn to positions outside of working with children in the classroom. We can't have it both ways. If we need leaders in our profession, we must be willing to help them develop and reward them. We must acknowledge the leadership that is already being provided at all levels of the profession, formally and informally.

What Is Leadership?

What is leadership and who are leaders? Leadership means different things to different people and is defined differently in different settings and environments. However, at least two common factors are evident in most definitions of leaders and leadership.

1. Leadership is a group phenomenon. At least two people must be involved—a leader must be leading someone.

2. Leadership usually involves intentional influence. At least one of the people involved must want to make something happen.

Given these two common factors, there are still a few more things to know about leadership. The development of leadership ability takes time. It is a lifelong process that begins at birth and an interactive process that is influenced by many factors including life and work experiences. Operating the most sought-after family child care center in your community, for example, doesn't happen in a day. When you first started out, you may not have had all the knowledge, information, and experience you needed. However, if you always got along well with younger children as a child, raised a number of children of your own, took a few classes in child development, or worked in a center for a while, you began to pull together many experiences that led you toward your goal. You learned different things from each experience, and you put them all together in a way that made sense to you. This process of integrating your experience gave you what you needed to begin your own family child care business. It made you a leader. And with more experiences, development, and learning comes a lot more leadership development!

SELF-SUFFICIENCY AND INTERDEPENDENCE

Effective leadership facilitates a person's or a group's growth in a way that encourages self-sufficiency *and* interdependence. Effective leadership creates self-sufficiency as we each work to make sure that everyone has an opportunity to contribute to the leadership process—growing into our own leadership potential and assisting others in growing into theirs. Effective leadership creates interdependence as we find ways to work together and draw on each others' unique gifts and strengths so we can accomplish common goals and achieve great things.

Take, for example, a new director who has just begun working in a child care center. She has a great vision for the future of the center and really wants to have more participation by the teachers in decisions that affect the center's overall work environment. Unfortunately, she also has a difficult time getting their "buy-in" for some of her ideas. The lead teacher does not have a lot of information about participatory decisions, but she really knows how to communicate with each teacher and has an uncanny knack for guessing exactly how each teacher will respond in a particular situation. By working together (interdependence) the director and the lead teacher can combine their skills to create a vision that meets all of their needs. In addition, both the director and the lead teacher are developing new leadership skills. The director is learning how to incorporate more ideas from others into her planning and the lead teacher is learning more about participatory decision making. In this process, each is becoming more self-sufficient.

MUTUAL INFLUENCE

Leadership includes the recognition of individual strengths and contributions as well as the recognition of individual responsibility in the leadership process. It is a subtle process of leaders and followers influencing each other. This process combines thoughts, beliefs, values, perspectives, expectations, feelings, and actions, and it causes leaders and followers to work collectively to achieve purposes and values they both share.

In your work with children, you can see how teachers and children constantly influence each other. Everything you do is modeled and transferred to young children as they learn by modeling and mimicking the adults around them. At the same time, children also have their own set of thoughts, beliefs, values, perspectives, expectations, feelings, and actions and causes. As children teach you what they want to have happen in their learning environment, you make adjustments so you can better meet their needs and hold their interest.

The process is similar for leaders and followers. Both followers and leaders have their own sets of thoughts, beliefs, values, and so on. A leader's actions are a model for the people who follow him and the followers are always learning from the leader. At the same time, a good leader is also learning from the others in the group what they want to have happen in the organization or on the project, and how they want it to happen. He uses this information to change policies, to revise the goals of the project, to rethink how he is leading.

Who Are Leaders?

Leaders are any individuals who influence others in a way that encourages them to higher or better performance and personal development. Effective leaders may or may not have authority, position, or status. They do, however, have integrity, dignity, and respect for others. Leaders empower, encourage, and support others in a shared effort to achieve

> Leadership includes the recognition of individual strengths and contributions as well as the recognition of individual responsibility in the leadership process. It is a subtle process of leaders and followers influencing each other.

goals or create change. Leaders can be found at all levels, in a variety of positions, within the many contexts of early childhood care and education. They take action where action is needed, and they enable others to take action when another person's strengths and ability are needed. Effective leaders care about other people. They see their relationship to and with others as essential to the overall strength and vitality of the group or organization. Effective leaders and effective leadership generate more leaders, thereby strengthening the leadership process itself.

Early childhood teachers are familiar with providing an encouraging, empowering, and supportive learning environment for children so each and every child has opportunities to learn.

This is how we strengthen the learning process. We can also provide this kind of leadership learning environment for each other by using our interactions with each other as an opportunity to encourage better performance and personal development. Veteran teachers can take newcomers under their wings and point out areas for growth and new learning. This is best done with a respect for the new teacher who is learning to master a new task and is still developing, much as when a child is learning to master a new task. Just like the child, the new teacher has the potential to master that task and teach it to someone else. This is how we generate more leaders and strengthen the leadership process.

> Leaders empower, encourage, and support others in a shared effort to achieve goals or create change.

How you see your role will influence what kind of leadership you bring to a situation. For example, leaders have been described as servants, those who go out ahead of the rest to show the way. Other words used to describe leaders are *architect, catalyst, advocate, prophet, mediator,* and *coach.* Leaders might be considered poets who look at their work settings from a variety of perspectives. Leaders can be designers and stewards who build communities in which people continually expand their capabilities. Leaders are learners, performers, power brokers, and role models. These words all describe leaders who play a primary role in making an organization or group better for its members. How you define your own role as a leader provides numerous clues as to how you perceive your relationship with children and their families.

Keep in mind the cultural values that influence what you think the role of a leader should be. In many African and African American communities, for example, great leaders have the twin roles of the *spokesperson* who voices the concerns of the community and the *follower* who is a true member of the community for whom she claims to speak. In an early childhood setting, an example of the twin roles of spokesperson and follower can be found in the political advocate who is an excellent spokesperson because she has been a teacher and understands the needs and challenges of the profession. However, she must also continue to be considered a member of the teaching community. That is, those teachers for whom she advocates must see her as one of them, as someone who follows their lead and perspective. This would be particularly true in the African and African American early childhood community, but it is an important concept to remember for any leadership setting.

ask yourself

Does one of the words used to describe leaders on pages 8 and 9 ring true for you and how you see your role in your work setting? What does your description mean in terms of your relationship and interactions with children? With their families?

Pick one of these words and describe how that role influences your relationship with the children and their families. For example, what does your work mean for children and families if you see yourself as an architect? What are you "building?" How will you "build" it? How will you know if what you are "building" meets the needs of the children and families you serve?

In what ways does your leadership provide others with opportunities to perform better and develop personally?

How do you know you are providing an encouraging, empowering, supportive environment? What would you look for in this kind of environment?

ask yourself

In what ways are the children you teach more likely to become teachers of their peers? In what ways are the teachers you lead more likely to become leaders of their peers?

In what ways do the least privileged in your group benefit? Think about the children in your classroom with the fewest resources (such as family, money, equipment, previous learning opportunities) or the newest teachers (new to the profession, new to your work setting). How does your leadership benefit them?

What cultural values influence your expectations of the role of a leader? How do your expectations compare with those of other cultural groups?

Other Terms Used to Discuss Leadership

One of the reasons there are so many definitions of effective leaders and leadership is that the use of other terms can be confusing. Terms that have often been used to discuss leadership include *power, authority, status,* and *management.* When these terms are used as a substitute for or in place of "leadership," people's feelings about the other four words affect how they feel about leadership. For example, someone who hears leadership equated with management might think of it as dull and boring, if that's the association they have with the word "management." In focusing on power, authority, status, and management we often make the mistake of placing leadership outside of the classroom or family child care setting. Let's look at what each of the four terms mean, particularly in relation to leadership.

POWER

Leadership is not mere *power*. Power, in its most casually accepted definition, can be described as an intentional, purposeful act in which one person uses some form of advantage in order to influence the behavior of another person. Power seems to be a "bad" word in early care and education. This may be because we are unfamiliar with the number of ways in which power can be used.

Power can be used on, for, or with another person. Power used *on* or *over* someone is simply oppression, since the "follower" is not provided with choices or options. Power used *for* someone is *facilitation*—opportunities, choices, and options are provided and the other person makes the decision. Power used *with* someone is *empowerment*—both you and the other person learn and succeed together, a very important part of leadership because each person can contribute unique gifts and abilities to accomplish a shared or common goal.

Terms that have often been used to discuss leadership include *power, authority, status,* and *management.*

AUTHORITY

Leadership is not simply having *authority*. A person in authority is the one who has the *right* to make certain decisions. This right may come from a variety of sources including an elected or appointed position, age (as in a family situation), or a professional position within a group or organization. A leader may possess authority, but a person in authority is not necessarily a leader. A person with authority may have the right to make a decision, but that doesn't mean he will make the right decision!

STATUS

Leadership is not the same as having *status*. People with status may be merely the people who occupy the top positions within an organization. Status doesn't always determine leadership ability. We all know that there are people who work at the top levels of every field who couldn't lead a group of five-year-olds to ice cream. All leaders have some form of status. Not all of those who have status can be called effective leaders.

MANAGEMENT

Is leadership the same as *management?* There remains an ongoing debate over the similarities and differences between leadership and management. For many, the two terms are interchangeable, just two different words to describe the same process. For others, however, there is a difference in the way leaders and managers perceive situations, interact with people, solve problems, and direct the group or organization. Leaders and managers can serve very different functions and purposes, but one without the other can be a setup for failure. The chart on the next page shows some of the ways in which leadership and management are different from each other.

　　To the children we care for, all grownups have authority, status, *and* power. How you use yours matters. I've spent some time explaining all of these terms because you will find them used often when people talk about leadership. As you think about your own leadership development, focus on what authority, status, and power you have; what each means to you; and how you tend to use them. The best leaders are those who tap the human desire to have some purpose in life. Increasingly, people look for purpose in the workplace and the best leaders assist them in fulfilling their potential.

MANAGEMENT	LEADERSHIP
Provides consistency and order	Produces forward movement in an organization
Keeps an operation on time and on budget over the long haul	Creates significant change
Provides the operating talent necessary to keep an organization focused on the day-to-day tasks that must be completed if objectives are to be met	Provides the conceptual talent necessary to see the historical perspective (both past and future) that facilitates growth, change, and innovation
Provides efficiency in climbing the ladder of success	Determines whether the ladder is leaning against the right wall

ask yourself

Think about a leadership situation in which you were involved or that you observed. Was the interaction based on power, authority, status, or management? How? From a leadership perspective, what might have made the outcome different?

How have you used power, authority, status, or management?

Describe a situation in which you used power on/over, power for, and power with. Why did you do it? What was the outcome? What was the other person's response?

Functions and Styles of Leadership

The functions of leadership should tell you and those around you what you want to have happen as a result of your leadership. The style of leadership you use should tell you and those around you the way in which you will carry out your leadership. The function is the goal of your leadership, the reason that the situation demands a leader. The style involves the methods you use to achieve your result.

Three leadership functions will be discussed below: 1) transformational leadership, which should change both the leader and the follower into better people and better leaders; 2) situational leadership, which should change as the leadership situation or needs change; and 3) servant leadership, which puts leaders in the position of serving others.

Two leadership styles will also be discussed below: 1) directive style, which involves a lot of instruction and guidance, and 2) a facilitative style, which involves acting only in a way that improves others.

Naturally, there are many more functions and styles of leadership. The ones discussed here provide examples and introduce you to some of the language and literature.

TRANSFORMATIONAL LEADERSHIP

Leadership can be transformational—changing, motivating, and elevating both the leaders and followers in ways that improve society and create an environment that prepares children and adults to participate in the leadership process. Transformational leaders are usually charismatic, inspirational, intellectually stimulating, and empathetic. To become a transformational leader, you must focus on your ability to influence and inspire others, to create change and provide a vision, and on your ability to work effectively with complexity, ambiguity, and uncertainty.

Transformational leadership is constantly needed, because you can't solve complex problems once and for all. The current transformational change becomes the new static pattern and today's solutions become tomorrow's problems. Keep this in mind as you develop your leadership ability. The change you create today will be great for solving today's problems, but tomorrow will bring new problems and the current solution will become obsolete.

ask yourself

Select a typical workday and review it from beginning to end. What are the specific events of the day that you would describe as transformational? How were these events transformational? Why were they?

What actions, behaviors, beliefs, and so on do you think increase your ability to transform yourself, others, and your work environment?

Think back on a problem that existed in your work environment a couple of years ago, one that resulted in a change in how things were done. In what ways has that change created a new set of problems or stopped working under the current circumstances?

If you could do just one thing to solve the new problem, what would that be? Why might it work?

SITUATIONAL LEADERSHIP

Leadership can be situational. Sometimes there are circumstances and factors in a given situation that determine who will emerge as a leader. Your leadership may emerge as a result of time, place, and circumstance. Rosa Parks is a familiar example. She chose an apt moment to put her years of leadership training and experience to work when she sat down in the front (whites-only section) of a bus. On that day her leadership was needed. The time, place, and circumstance called for her to rise to the occasion. Once you experience effective leadership in one situation, you'll find it easier to recognize other leadership opportunities and you'll be more comfortable taking on increased leadership roles.

ask yourself

Think about a situation where an immediate decision was needed and you were the only one available to make it.

How did you feel?

What thoughts went through your mind?

Did you make the decision? If yes, describe the steps that led to the decision. If no, describe why not.

What would you do differently now? Why?

SERVANT LEADERSHIP

Leadership can be serving. Servant leaders in early childhood education are those who see themselves as serving coworkers, children, and their families. Servant leaders do not focus as much on their own needs and goals; they focus on the needs and goals of others. If your family child care program, for example, is designed to meet your personal goals and fulfill your personal vision, that can be a form of leadership, but it is not servant leadership. If your family child care program is designed to meet the goals and visions of the families who leave their children in your care, that is servant leadership. A servant leader can be the official head of a child care setting or simply the one who keeps all of you on a path toward the goal you all hope to achieve. Becoming a servant leader or a servant follower is not an easy process. It requires that each of us determine what actions and behaviors are most likely to benefit those who are being served and that the least fortunate of those served perceive themselves better off as a result of those actions and behaviors.

ask yourself

In what ways does your early child care program serve coworkers, children, and their families?

How do you lead and serve children and their families?

How well served are the least privileged children and families in your work setting?

DIRECTIVE LEADERSHIP

Your leadership *style* is the process you use to monitor, guide, coach, direct, and evaluate the work of others. Your leadership style, much like your teaching style, will be greatly influenced by your values and beliefs about how people (children and adults) grow, develop, and change.

A directive leadership style often is used when an individual or group is performing some new task. As with children learning a new task, much direction, guidance, monitoring, and feedback are needed. You need to be involved in the task almost as much as the child. The same is true of a directive leadership style when interacting with adults. If a coworker is learning a new task, you will need to spend almost as much time on the task as the learner. Step-by-step instructions, watching as the task is being performed the first few times, feedback on the learner's progress and helpful changes are all methods used in a directive leadership style.

This is similar to a classroom in which the teacher provides some direction and guidance as well as opportunities for children to develop internal monitoring and responsibility. The trick is to determine if this style is something you use all the time, which makes it a style, or if it is something you use only until the learner has mastered the task, which makes it a part of the situational leadership function.

An authoritarian style may look similar to a directive one, but it focuses primarily on the completion of the task, sometimes at the expense of the learner's needs. Someone who uses this type of "authority-obedience" style gives orders, not advice, and expects those orders to be carried out without question or hesitation. In a classroom, an authoritarian teacher presents the information or content expecting that the child will learn without question or hesitation. Most of us have been in situations where someone talked or gave a lecture with no learner interaction or participation and then had the nerve to call it teaching! An authoritarian leadership style is seen among adults in the military, where people are often expected to follow orders from a supervisor or commanding officer without question or discussion.

> The facilitative style focuses on the individual strengths of each person, and encourages and develops leadership ability in each.

FACILITATIVE LEADERSHIP

A facilitative leadership style involves providing group members with the means, resources, authority, and responsibility to act in the best interest of those affected by the task. A facilitative style is never authoritarian; it may be directive and always meets the needs of coworkers, children, and their families—much like servant leadership. The facilitative style focuses on the individual strengths of each person, and encourages and develops leadership ability in each. The facilitative teacher is, of course, similar—providing children with the means, resources, and authority to be active participants in the teaching/learning process while understanding her role as learner and the children's roles as teachers. Emergent curriculum comes to mind in a facilitative teaching environment. Emergent curriculum occurs when the teacher uses the emerging interests, questions, and skills of the children to modify and change the teacher's original plan. Facilitative leadership occurs in a similar way when leaders look for and use the emerging interests, questions, and skills of others as focus points for increasing leadership.

Think about how you can vary your leadership function and style to meet the needs or experience level of your coworkers. People who are new to a job or who are performing a new task may need more monitoring, guidance, and direction. A directive leadership style is appropriate for them in that situation. Those who have been performing a task for a long time may do better left on their own to do what they do best. A facilitative leadership style will probably work better for them. Coworkers may need extra opportunities to learn new perspectives and understand new values and priorities. They may need more time for their ideas and beliefs to form or change. When you look at leadership, remember that there is no one best way to lead. Instead, you must adapt your leadership function and style to the needs of the group. This, of course, is exactly the same as taking a developmental approach to children's learning. Developmentally appropriate practice applies to leadership as well!

Leadership Development and Human Development

Leadership development, human development, and life experiences are interrelated processes that help make us who we are. Human development is the process by which we change cognitively, socially, intellectually, and physically as we mature. Leadership development is the process by which we increase our ability to create and influence change, growth, and achievement. Life experiences are those factors, events, circumstances, and so forth that define who we are as individuals and influence how we see the world.

Human development and leadership development both involve an evolution, a transformation that changes who we are over time. This change is both qualitative and quantitative. Through your life experiences, you do not simply add to the number of things you know or can do, but the quality of what you know or can do becomes different. When a child learns to dress himself, he learns, over time, how to put on a shirt, underwear, pants, socks, and shoes. This is *quantity*. He also learns, over time, how to dress more neatly or to coordinate his clothing. This is *quality*.

Much like human development, becoming a leader is a developmental process and requires you to create and interpret your own life experiences and knowledge. Some early childhood theorists call this "constructivism." Like human development, leadership development takes time and is never finished. Leadership development is individual—it differs depending on personality, life stage, and other circumstances. Who you are as a leader is an integration of your previous and current selves and the new you that will continue to emerge as you learn, grow, and gain experience. You will discover and invent your own way of leading. In many ways, you have no other choice. You are a unique individual. No other person can be you better than you can.

Your beliefs and theories about how people learn and grow, and the primary factors that affect their development, will influence your beliefs and theories about leadership development. As you think about leadership development, you will have to clarify your theories as a teacher and as a leader. Your ability to articulate your beliefs to others will increase your thoughtfulness, your intent, your consistency, and your results.

ask yourself

You may be very familiar with the concept of a teachable moment and emergent curriculum. Think about how you would recognize, take advantage of, or provide a "lead-able" moment. How might facilitative leadership be worked into what you do?

How will your leadership development be affected by your beliefs and theories about how children grow and learn?

ASSIMILATION AND ACCOMMODATION

Child development provides useful examples for making links with leadership development. For example, children use assimilation and accommodation when confronted with new knowledge. They *assimilate* new knowledge when they first learn that not every four-legged animal is a "doggie." Their knowledge begins to *accommodate* new knowledge when they develop a second category for four-legged animals, "cow." Over the years, children assimilate and accommodate many times in order to understand the multitude of four-legged animals that exist in the world.

Through our own processes of assimilation and accommodation, we can transfer our current knowledge around child development to our emerging knowledge around leadership development. Multitasking, coordinating different senses, and developing competency over time are just three examples of teaching skills that translate into leadership skills. As each is discussed below, think about what you already do well as a teacher and how you can use those same skills as a leader.

Multitasking

Multitasking takes place when you engage in more than one activity at the same time, when you make use of more than one skill simultaneously. Some teachers think they are not good at multitasking, but in reality most people are experts at it. They have just become so proficient at something that they fail to remember that it requires doing more than one action or using more than one skill. Take learning to write a paragraph in English. Children must make simultaneous use of many skills: remembering the correct symbol (letter) used to make a specific sound, choosing correctly between similar looking symbols (such as *b, d, p,* and *q*), putting the symbols in a specific order so they represent correctly spelled words, and focusing on the idea or story they are telling as they put several words together in sentences. Most children can do all of these things simultaneously and quickly by age eight. By the time we are adults, we can perform the multiple tasks involved in writing and reading so quickly that we come to see writing and reading as one fluid task.

Leadership is about multitasking. In any leadership situation, we must simultaneously think about the purpose of our actions and how those actions relate to the goals and directions of the group; we must balance the needs and relationships of the people involved with needs and requirements of the tasks to be completed; and we must be able to hold

> Being patient with your developing competency will also be critical to your leadership development.

our vision of the future while focusing on what needs to be done today. As with reading and writing, the goal in leadership development is to perform these multiple tasks so quickly that leadership becomes one fluid process.

Coordinating different senses

Children coordinate many different senses as they play and explore their world. They taste the toy and develop a sense of what it feels like both orally and manually. They see the toy and listen to the sounds it makes as it is tasted and held. They smell the toy and they experience a feeling of satisfaction and happiness with the whole event. As adults, we coordinate many different senses when we take in a leadership situation. We see the dynamics and individual facial and body expressions of other people. We sense the energy of the group or individual, or the situation, in which they find themselves. We hear both the words and the tone of what is being said. Much like coordinating different senses, the ability to coordinate different leadership skills allows us to achieve great accomplishments or master new skills.

Developing competency over time

Being patient with your developing competency will also be critical to your leadership development. Children feel good about themselves and their abilities when they believe they are competent at doing the things that are important to them and when they believe they can compete equally with their peers. Feelings of incompetence come when children repeatedly fail at something or when they are told that they aren't capable of doing something. A very perceptive and bright child once described the difference between gifted and special education. In the gifted classes, teachers find out what you are good at and let you do it again and again and again. In the special education classes, teachers find out what you can't do and make you do it over and over.

Feelings of competence and incompetence are related to your leadership development. You will feel incompetent at some skills while you are practicing and learning. Reflection will be key. As you repeat various skills and learn new ones, think about the end result, the consequences of your words and actions.

ask yourself

Did things turn out the way you expected? Are you getting better? Can you tell?

When do you feel competent? Is it when you believe that others think you are capable of succeeding? Why do you feel that way?

When do you feel incompetent? Is it when you believe that others do not think you are capable of succeeding? Why do you feel that way?

Think about the natural stages of development as you build or construct your knowledge of leadership practice and take baby steps in your leadership development journey. Just as babies understand words long before they can actually talk, you will understand many leadership concepts long before you may be able to apply them. Your first attempts may feel like baby talk (such as "all broke," "me bite," or "kitty bye-bye"). With practice and patience, your leadership attempts will become more complex (such as "The cup is broken," "I bit the apple," or "The cat is gone"). At some point, you will arrive at the "adolescent" stage of leadership. Through our knowledge of childhood and adolescent development, we know that there are various stages at which humans strive to construct an identity—a clear understanding of who we are, why we are, and how we want to be in the world. The same holds true in the developmental process of becoming a leader. At that stage, it may be helpful to ask yourself the following questions:

- Who am I as a leader?
- What am I good at?
- What do I believe in?
- What groups do I belong to?
- What do others think of me?
- What do I believe about what they think?

The details of our individual lives are a constant part of each learning environment and each leadership environment. Education and learning are social processes that can be used to maintain or change the status quo. In the same way, leadership can be used to domesticate people to do as instructed or to liberate people to critique situations and circumstances and make decisions for themselves. Who you are and who you become as a leader will be evident in how the others (adults and children) grow and change as a result of your role in the leadership process.

Developing Your Personal Definition of Leadership

In the end, how you define leaders and leadership will not be nearly as important as how others are affected by who you are and what you do. Others will come to know your definition of a leader and leadership by the results and consequences of their interactions with you over time. How will they define you? Your thinking about leadership will become the basis for how you make decisions and what you expect of others.

Don't be too concerned about deciding which single leadership function or style is perfect for you. Just as you would use a combination of strategies to inform your work with children, you'll need a combination of strategies to inform your leadership. The most perfect leader is composed of all the leadership functions and styles put together. Because leadership is a complex, dynamic, interactive, situational process, there is no "one best way" to develop or strengthen the many skills, abilities, and competencies needed. Those who will be most able to respond in a variety of leadership situations (such as curriculum quality, political analysis, family involvement, mentoring, creative problem solving) will be those who have taken advantage of a variety of leadership opportunities (such as classes, role models, volunteer experiences, books, observations, reflection). As time and experience add up, your leadership skill and ability will transform into a whole new leadership strength that is uniquely yours.

> Just as you would use a combination of strategies to inform your work with children, you'll need a combination of strategies to inform your leadership.

ask yourself

What is your definition of a leader? Of leadership? How did you arrive at this definition?

summary

This chapter has introduced you to some basic concepts around the definitions, roles, and challenges of leaders and leadership. Various leadership functions and styles and how they look in the leadership process have also been discussed. Through your examination of leadership development and human development, you have had numerous opportunities to begin reflecting on how to make links between the two and to begin the process of transferring your skill and ability from one arena to another. In chapter 2, you will look even deeper into who you are and how you learn to be a leader. What role does family play in the development of leadership strength and ability? How do your life experiences and your culture combine to create a leader who is uniquely you? Chapter 2 will cover all of this and provide ideas for how you can stretch yourself.

story time

Tilman is the teacher in the toddler room and has just begun working with a new assistant, seventeen-year-old Lori. These first few days with Lori have been a little frustrating for Tilman because Lori seems to need a lot of guidance and direction and there is really no time for that, what with so many active young-sters. On the third day, Tilman goes home and plops tiredly onto her couch.

"Tough day?" asks her husband.

"Yeah," Tilman replies. "I wish Lori would just go do what I tell her to do instead of asking me questions about what to do all day long!"

"Must be like working with a two-year-old," her husband responds.

Tilman thinks about that for the rest of the evening. The next day at work, Tilman approaches Lori in a whole new way. Her husband was right. Working with someone who is new to a position *is* like working with a two-year-old. Lori is simply in the early developmental stages of learning about her new job and her role, and early developmental stages require guidance, modeling, and direction until the behavior is internalized. Tilman needs to adjust her style to accommodate Lori's situation, or her level of "maturity" in this new role. After two or three days of intense supervision by Tilman, Lori is off and running on her own and feels competent to do what is expected of her.

more reading

Bass, Bernard. 1990. *Bass and Stogdill's handbook of leadership: Theory, research, and managerial applications.* New York: The Free Press.

Etzioni, Amitai. 1991. *A responsive society: Collected essays on guiding deliberate social change.* San Francisco: Jossey-Bass Publishers.

Greenleaf, Robert K. 1977. *Servant leadership: A journey into the nature of legitimate power and greatness.* New York: Paulist Press.

Kagan, Sharon L., and Barbara T. Bowman, ed. 1997. *Leadership in early care and education.* Washington, D.C.: National Association for the Education of Young Children.

Samovar, Larry A., and Richard E. Porter, ed. 1997. *Intercultural communication: A reader.* Belmont, Calif.: Wadsworth Publishing Company.

T'Shaka, Oba. 1990. *The art of leadership.* Richmond, Calif.: Pan African Publications.

CHAPTER 2

Who, Me, a Leader?

This chapter is designed to help you reflect on the following:

- The ways in which your own skills and abilities were influenced by your family experience

- The ways in which you as a parent or adult family member develop and use leadership skills and abilities in your interactions with children

- The ways in which culture, life experiences, and learning preferences influence the type of leadership skills you develop

- The ways in which good leadership and good teaching require the same kinds of skills, competencies, and characteristics

Family As a Context for Leadership

You would be surprised at how early you began developing your leadership ability! Many people wonder whether leaders are born or made. Do strong leaders possess those genes and family dynamics that set them up for future leadership potential, or do potential leaders evolve as a result of life experiences combined with leadership development and training? Leaders are both born and made. They develop as a combination of both. We were all born with some natural strengths, gifts, and abilities—things we do effortlessly without giving them much thought. On the other hand, we all have skills and abilities that are the result of practice, hard work, and training. Most leaders find that their greatest achievements and most effectiveness come when they use a combination of both natural ability and trained skill.

> Many of the leadership characteristics and strengths that come naturally to you were evident in your childhood.

Why is it important to understand how you develop and use leadership in the family environment? All of us take into the workplace the skills and abilities we learned as a result of growing up in a family situation. Many people don't know how the leadership styles and skills they use in their interactions with family members relate to leadership on the job, but the connection is there anyway. If we are to strengthen and develop the best of these skills, it is necessary to first understand that we have them. Making the relationship between leadership at home and leadership at work more apparent helps us strengthen those skills that are effective and to recognize areas for growth.

An important point to remember about family is that all types of families can supply the components necessary for a flourishing, functioning family environment that results in healthy, happy children if there is access to the resources and services they need. "Family," as used in this book, will refer to married, heterosexual parents and children; single mothers and fathers; single parents cohabitating; gay and lesbian couples with children; adult singles or couples and their parents (or other older relatives); singles or couples raising their grandchildren or the children of relatives; older siblings raising younger siblings; foster parents with unrelated children; or circles of friends who consider themselves a family. Any of these kinds of families can raise children effectively. Children and adults from all of these kinds of families display leadership strengths and skills.

Many of the leadership characteristics and strengths that come naturally to you were evident in your childhood. The following questions will help you think about your strengths.

ask yourself

As a child, were you described as achievement-oriented? Did people find you to be sociable, reliable, or encouraging?

What leadership skills and abilities seem to come to you naturally?

What leadership skills and abilities have you been working on, practicing, or studying?

Think about your own family experience growing up. What strengths and skills did you begin to develop as a young child? What was always a challenge for you?

List three childhood characteristics that seemed to come naturally to you. How can each one add to your leadership skill and ability today?

How a family is structured and what place an individual has in her family also affects how she might show leadership. Birth order and family size, economics, culture, and expectations are all factors that can affect a person's leadership.

BIRTH ORDER AND FAMILY SIZE

First- and last-born children tend to show more leadership ability early on. First-born children often benefit from the early, more personal interaction with adults and adult language, and they are more likely to be given more responsibility and are expected to mature faster. This is particularly true with the oldest girl in low-income families or families with working mothers. My own childhood serves as an example. As the oldest of six children, I was expected to help my mother (a stay-at-home) with the younger children. My first baby-sitting responsibility came at age six! When my mother needed to run to the store (just two blocks away), she would put my younger siblings in front of the television. I sat behind them. Their job was to watch television. My job was to watch them.

Youngest children, on the other hand, tend to be more disobedient and more persistent, and are often disregarded when family or personal decisions are made. Because of this, youngest children often challenge the status quo, persist in their efforts to change things, and insist on being a part of a decision-making team later in life. As leaders, youngest children tend to take more notice of how they are (or are not) involved in making the decisions and when their input is blocked or ignored. They are also more persistent in having clear processes in place that keep power distributed between the members of a team. As leaders, the youngest children of larger families are more likely to try new and different things. This is the result of rarely having the opportunity to be the first in the family to do something (such as take first steps, ride a bike, learn to whistle). By the time the third or fourth child learns to whistle, the novelty has worn off for parents, so these children grow up eager to be the first to do something praiseworthy or interesting.

Middle children tend to show more variety in their leadership development, depending on the gender and age configurations of their family. In families where the middle child is the only girl and particularly if she is closer in age to her older brother, she will take on more of the characteristics of "the oldest girl." If she is closer in age to her younger brother, she could also take on more characteristics of "the youngest," especially if the family environment tends to be more patriarchal. Many middle children, however, are just that—not the youngest and not the oldest. Middle children tend to be more adventuresome, often take more risks, and exhibit more independent behavior as a result of their need to establish an identity based on something other than *not* being oldest or youngest. As leaders, middle children are likely to try on different roles and demonstrate leadership flexibility, using the same skills to shift roles as they did in childhood.

The size of your family also influenced your leadership development. Children with three or four siblings tend to work better in groups attempting to achieve a group goal. Those from smaller or larger families are more inclined to work better on an individual basis for an individual goal.

ask yourself

Are you the oldest, the only, the youngest, or in the middle? What leadership skills did you learn because of this? What are the leadership challenges you face because of birth order? Which leadership skills do you share in common with your siblings? Which skills are different? Why do you think this is so?

How has family size influenced your leadership development?

FAMILY CULTURE

The more you understand the leadership implications of culture and other differences, the easier it will become for you to "make room" for other perspectives in your work with children. In many ways, the more you understand and create diversity, the easier your work becomes as children, families, communities, and coworkers increase their collaborative efforts with you.

Culture influences the expectations and roles emphasized within the family and the family's relationship to the larger community. For example, the strong kinship bonds and mother-child relationships of African families are evident in the strong role of the mother or grandmother in African American culture. For many Asians and Asian Americans, family and community needs may take priority over the needs of an individual. In more traditional Native families, the concepts of ownership and sharing are markedly different from the European-American perspective. In each of these communities and many others, these cultural influences will determine both parental and leadership expectations and roles.

The historical experiences of the cultural group also play a role in leadership development within the family. Cultures that have been subjected to oppression or socioeconomic injustice result in more collective and collaborative family groups, such as the pooling of resources practiced by immigrant groups. These experiences can result in the pooling of leadership resources as well. Leadership is more likely to be shared, and children skilled in collaboration and community building are more likely to have leadership opportunities. Caregiving tasks are also shared, especially in cultures where families are separated by slavery, economics, war, or death. Children living in oppression learn particular leadership skills from these circumstances, including trust, courage, dependability, empathy, and integrity. Parents begin early on teaching children how to recognize these traits and characteristics as part of basic survival skills. Understanding the differences will increase your ability to understand the context in which leadership in families develops. Families in different circumstances will foster and focus on different leadership skills. When families from different cultural and historical experiences come together in the workplace, they bring a diverse set of skills to the leadership process.

Culture also influences the ways in which adults and children interact with each other. A "good" parent may be expected to tend to a crying baby immediately or to wait to see if the fussiness passes. A "good" parent may be expected to engage in much physical play with a child or to engage in quiet, less physical activities. A "good" parent may also be expected to do all of the above depending on the situation. As you continue to think about what it means to be a "good" leader and teacher of young children, keep in mind that there are many ways to be a good leader and many ways to interact with children and adults. Paying attention to what makes a "good" leader in a number of cultures will help you increase your own leadership skill and ability.

There are also challenges and differing opinions over children's ethnic socialization if they are not members of the dominant cultural group. Some feel that children should be taught the values, skills, abilities, and behaviors that will help them fit in better with the dominant culture. For others, it is better to ensure that children maintain historical cultural traditions that help them to be model citizens within their cultural group and community. And, of course, still others are more inclined toward biculturalism for their children—helping them become empowered members of both cultural groups. Our role,

> When families from different cultural and historical experiences come together in the workplace, they bring a diverse set of skills to the leadership process.

as developing leaders, is to understand a variety of cultural family interaction patterns and the impact on our leadership skill, ability, and strengths. The families and communities served by your early childhood program have their own family leadership experiences and expectations and may expect a certain kind of leadership from you. Part of your leadership development will be increasing your understanding of the many ways in which a family's cultural expectations influence its leadership expectations.

ask yourself

What have you learned about leadership in the family through your culture? Through your group's or your community's historical experience?

Adults of different cultures also vary in the ways that they communicate and interact with adults and peers, and others. What communication and interaction skills have you learned from your culture? What's missing?

In your own family, what cultural leadership skills have you learned? What are you passing on to the next generation?

How do your teaching practices reflect the children's home communities and their expectations for their children?

FAMILY EXPECTATIONS

Families play an essential role as the birthplace for potential leadership. So many of our current leadership characteristics, skills, and abilities had their beginnings in our families. Some examples are confidence, self-esteem, and assertiveness—important characteristics for recognizing leadership opportunities and being able to take advantage of them. Each of these characteristics may develop early in children, but may be specific to certain situations. As a child, you may have been confident in one area and not in another or confident with one group of people, but not with another. If you grew up in a family that spoke a language other than English, you may have had more confidence and been more assertive expressing your feelings at home than at school. You were still developing leadership skills you would use as an adult, but may have used those skills more with one group (family) than with another (school).

The family can set the expectations for the children's achievements and success, in both positive and negative ways, making it possible for children from very different family environments to develop the same leadership traits. For example, the motivation to lead and succeed may result from a) a very loving, praising home life that stresses risk taking, b) a home with never-ending high expectation and very little love, or c) a home where a child was told she wouldn't amount to much so she had to succeed just to prove her family wrong! Look for and cultivate the leadership potential in each and every family experience regardless of the family circumstances. You never know where a future leader may emerge.

The absence or presence of confidence, self-esteem, and assertiveness also influences the roles children play or avoid and, therefore, the leadership they assert as adults. The process of developing leadership characteristics, skills, and ability begins in the family, but becomes more active as children are exposed to divergent or conflicting viewpoints and experiences outside the family in child care centers, schools, community and religious organizations, and within the context of their culture.

ask yourself

Where did you find confidence as a child? Where was your confidence lacking? Below are some suggestions to get you started. Add more of your own.

art	inventing things	creating games
math	science experiments	giving advice
caring for pets	swimming	caring for others
drama/pretend play	biking	basketball
school work	jumping rope	
storytelling	learning languages	

People want to hear what potential leaders have to say and what they think. When you were young, in what ways did other children or adults listen to you or seek out your opinions and advice?

Parenting and Leading

Strong connections can be made between what leaders do and what adults who have or work with children do. What is parenting? Simply put, parenting is the way we prepare children to meet the expectations and challenges of their communities and society as a whole and to understand the social and cultural ways of the times. If you do not have children, you still influence, through teaching and example, how children are prepared to become members of their communities and society.

The concept of parent leadership assumes that all parents are leaders for their children, using a complex set of leadership knowledge and skills. Not every parent is born with this leadership ability, and most do not gain it immediately when they become responsible for a child. The role of the parent as a family leader is a dynamic process of human development for both the adults and the children. Parents and children grow and change together, supporting and challenging each other as they play out their lives together.

ask yourself

Potential leaders think about their natural gifts and talents, what they do best. What do you do best? What natural gifts and talents do you possess? How do you use them? Why or why not?

Ask your children what they think are your leadership strengths and weaknesses. Ask them what they think theirs are.

In the big picture of parenting, many leadership functions are performed: finding and organizing resources; cultivating their children's intellect, interests, and talents; setting expectations for their children's successes; influencing their children's self-esteem through demonstrations of love and praise; providing basic necessities such as food and shelter; and ensuring adequate health care, quality child care, a good education, and a safe environment. In many ways, parents serve as the first "case managers" for their children, responsible for finding, organizing, and managing all the resources their children need for healthy development physically, socially, cognitively, and emotionally.

On a daily basis, parents use a variety of leadership skills and strategies with their children and other family members. Consider the following list of leadership tasks. Give one example of how you have used each.

- **Planning** activities and events for family gatherings or outings

- Creating **team-building** activities to strengthen family bonds

- **Negotiating** with the children and other family members to reach agreements

- **Scheduling** the day to accommodate the children's school and recreational activities

- **Modeling** appropriate behavior based on family values and preferences

- **Arbitrating** disagreements between siblings

- **Setting goals** in order to afford a family vacation

- **Supervising** the children in their work, play, and interactions with others

- **Setting performance expectations** for the children's chores and behavior

- **Motivating** the children and other family members to accomplish tasks

- Understanding how **group dynamics** influence how family members respond to each other

- Using **problem-solving** strategies to help the children figure out what went wrong with a project

- **Making decisions** based on current information or past results

- **Strategizing** ways to get through tough times

- Using **multitasking skills** to cook dinner, supervise homework, and get one more load of laundry done, all at the same time

By substituting "leader" for "parent" and "employee" for "child," you can begin to see the parallels between leadership in the workplace and leadership in parenting. Parents use leadership styles in their families in much the same way as other leaders do.

Compare, for example, the parent who views a child's questions as a sign of disrespect with the supervisor who reprimands an employee for asking too many questions. Compare, on the other hand, the parent who involves the child in solving a family problem with the supervisor who involves employees in the problem-solving process.

FAMILY LEADERSHIP STYLES

Let's take a look at three families camping together. The first set of parents use what seems to be a "laissez-faire," or hands-off, style of leadership resulting in family members doing whatever they feel like doing. The children run free and there are no structures, rules, or guidelines. In contrast, the second set of parents may use a "participative" style of leadership. All family members have a part in all their activities, which are done collectively with guidelines and set boundaries. The third set of parents use an "authoritarian" style. They determine activities and assign tasks without a lot of input from the children and expect tasks to be completed effectively and efficiently.

The three styles are very different and reflect different ideas that families have about what makes a fun camping experience. The first set of parents thinks camping is fun because all rules have been put aside. The second set thinks camping is fun because it allows parents and children to spend time together and learn to work as a team. The third set thinks camping is fun because everything is organized and efficient. The leadership provided by each set of parents is designed to meet the goals and values they have set for their families. As you can see, the style of leadership can be very diverse, even when the goal is the same: have fun while camping.

Different parenting styles are influenced by culture and community as well. "Hands-off" parenting may be used to encourage children to discover their environment for themselves, may be a desire to raise self-reliant children, or may simply be used only in certain situations, such as camping. Parenting that is "shared" with children may be the result of an egalitarian society in which all have a say or may be the desire of an individual to raise fully empowered children. Firm, directive parenting is often the result of surviving in an oppressive society or of maintaining traditional values of respect and obedience. The important point to remember is that different parenting styles reflect different leadership styles and involve different leadership skills, which parents implement in the rearing and socialization of the young.

ask yourself

What was the leadership style used in your family when you were growing up? What was the impact of this on your own leadership development? What leadership style do you use in your current family? What is the impact of this on each family member?

How did your family's theory of child development and how kids should be raised affect your leadership development?

Think about the family of a childhood friend. In what ways were your two families different? In what ways were they alike? What leadership skills and abilities do you think were developing in your friend's family?

Think for a moment about how each of these leadership styles (hands-off, participative, and authoritarian) might look in the ECE workplace. What might be the positive aspects of each style? What might be the negative aspects of each style?

The parent who provides meaningful assistance and guidance to a child so that the child will do well in school and be admitted to college performs tasks similar to the lead teacher who assists an aide in developing new skills in order to become a classroom teacher. The parent who successfully manages the family budget performs tasks similar to a family child care provider who is responsible for ensuring that her budget stays on track. It is clear that the many duties and tasks performed by parents coincide with those performed by leaders in other areas. Parents have the opportunity to "grow" leaders in much the same way as people working in other organizations.

Good Teachers Make Good Leaders

Faced with a situation that demands leadership, a good teacher will often display the characteristics and skills of a good leader. Like any other leader, the teacher understands that change is inevitable and that there will always be challenges. Both teacher and leader see the opportunities and benefits in taking risks and learning from past mistakes. Both constantly reflect on their actions and beliefs and think about the results and consequences of each. Both teacher and leader understand the importance of teaching, learning, and achieving as part of a community. These basic dispositions add to the creation of an environment in which learning and leading happen naturally, developmentally. As you develop as a leader, pay attention to the characteristics, skills, and behaviors you use as a teacher and think about how this impacts your effectiveness. On the next page is a comparison of teaching competencies and the competencies we generally agree all leaders in the field of early childhood care and education must possess, both to lead and to manage an effective and efficient team. Describe how you achieve the competencies in each column. Have someone else describe how you achieve the competencies in each column. You may be surprised at the result!

EFFECTIVE ECE **LEADER** COMPETENCIES	EFFECTIVE ECE **TEACHER** COMPETENCIES
Creation and Development of Organizational Culture	
1 Articulates organizational mission, goals, and direction; plans small wins; is a capable tribal storyteller (transmits the organization's culture); and envisions the future	Understands the curriculum and can explain it to many people in many different ways; recognizes the small steps; is involved, honest, and sincere in motives; is assertive, energetic; shows commitment or passion
Written and Verbal Communication Skills	
2 Builds networks, knows about cultural differences, builds teams, supports others, manages conflict	Is people-oriented, a good listener, and a good public speaker; shows consideration of others, commitment or passion, sociability, and a sense of humor
Analytic Problem-Solving Skills	
3 Monitors, informs, clarifies, seeks opportunities	Balances action, theory, and reflection through a combination of work, study, and thought; is open to new perspectives; explains a problem from more than one perspective; takes risks; shows courage
Interpersonal Skills	
4 Motivates and inspires others, fosters collaboration, resolves conflict, recognizes and rewards others for their achievements	Is people-oriented, honest, and sincere; shows consideration of others, understanding of followers, sociability, and a sense of humor

EFFECTIVE ECE **LEADER** COMPETENCIES	EFFECTIVE ECE **TEACHER** COMPETENCIES
Attitudes / Dispositions	
5 Shows flexibility, openness to change, openness to contrary opinion; accommodates divergent viewpoints; experiments; takes risks	Shows consistency and endurance; is enthusiastic, yet humble; shows self-confidence or self-esteem; able to accommodate divergent viewpoints; takes risks and shows courage
Child and Family Development Knowledge	
6 Knows about multiple intelligences and learning styles; knows about different cultural perspectives regarding developmental values and priorities	Recognizes differences and similarities; recognizes talent in others; shows self-confidence or self-esteem; shows consideration of others; can accommodate divergent viewpoints
Fiscal Management and Planning	
7 Knows about budgets; can find and allocate resources	Shows foresight, good judgment; is honest and sincere in motives; shows consistency and endurance; is energetic or active; takes risks and shows courage
Staff Development and Supervision	
8 Problem solves, consults, is capable of telling *why* rather than *how*, delegates, plans and organizes	Recognizes differences and similarities; recognizes talent in others; is enthusiastic, yet humble; shows consideration of others; can accommodate divergent viewpoints; understands followers

Some people come by the things on these lists naturally while others have to be intentional in developing and using them. It does not matter whether you come by a leadership or teaching characteristic or ability naturally or have to work at it. What matters is that you engage in each one. As with any new skill, leadership must be attempted and practiced if it is to be developed.

ask yourself

Refer to the chart on the previous pages. In what ways do you practice the eight competencies naturally? Where do you need to stretch? How? What is your stretching plan?

You may not be able to imagine yourself as the ideal ECE leader using all of the competencies and skills described above. Instead, think about how many of them you do use and what you need to work on next. Certain characteristics, experiences, values, attributes, and competencies directly influence the possibility that you will emerge as a leader within a group. The more skills, abilities, and perspectives you have, the more opportunities you will have to emerge as a leader. Persist and be patient with your leadership development, and find opportunities to practice as many of the competencies as you can. To develop, practice, and strengthen these is to place yourself in the position of gaining a new leadership ability when the opportunity arises.

How Adults Learn

The process by which you *acquire* leadership skill and ability is just as important as the leadership skill or ability itself. How you learn matters just as much as what you are learning. There are lots of ways to learn leadership: storytelling, rhymes, reading, practice, movement, songs, classes, books, listening to the story of a colleague, observing someone else, workshops, trial and error, reflection, dialogue with others, and many more. Just as learning must be presented in a number of ways if it is to be remembered, leadership development must take place in a number of ways in order to make our leadership ability more complex and flexible, and in order to make it "stick." Creative play is vital to children's cognitive development and is an important part of leadership as well. Play in leadership means being creative, flexible, and curious; thinking of possibilities; and taking chances. It means taking on new roles, just as children do in pretend play.

As early childhood professionals, we know that children learn best when they are following their own interests, when they can make choices, when they have hands-on experience, and when they can interact with others. Adults learn best under much the same circumstances, and this type of learning environment is also best for leadership development. Real growth and learning take place in the midst of confusion, excitement, disequilibrium, reflection, and practice. Children experience assimilation (hooking new knowledge to previous knowledge) and accommodation (reconstructing previous knowledge as a result of new knowledge) as they learn. The same will happen to you during your leadership development. Your previous ability will provide the links that make sense of your new skill and ability. As you become more practiced and proficient, your previous leadership ability and skill will change into something completely new and different.

Leadership opportunities should have elements of both familiarity and novelty. The familiarity of the situation provides a level of comfort and competence. The process of assimilation makes it possible to link the new situation to previous learning, to something we already know or are able to do. The novelty of the situation provides the growing edge, the opportunity to make choices and decisions. The process of accommodating this newness allows for the construction of new knowledge and the reconstruction of previous knowledge. We adjust our previous knowledge in order to understand something new and different. We all have "knowledge" and "facts" that are not as accurate as we might think. Just as children have to learn and unlearn a lot as they add to their knowledge/experience base, adults have a lot to learn and unlearn about leadership and what it means to lead.

As we learn, we create categories, little boxes, to put the learning in. Each experience, event, idea, action, and fact is placed in a category with other items that are similar. Learning needs to be both relevant and connected for learners of all ages. If what you are learning doesn't seem to have any relevance to or connection with anything in your life or your previous knowledge, the learning will not "stick." It simply will not seem important to you, and you will not remember it. Then, later, when something happens to you that makes that learning relevant to your life, you'll have that familiar experience: "I remember someone told me something about that once, but I can't remember what it was." Now the learning is relevant and connected. Now you will learn it and remember it. Leadership is the same way. You will learn and remember best those leadership concepts that are relevant to and connected with your experiences and your previous knowledge.

As early childhood professionals, we know that children learn best when they are following their own interests, when they can make choices, when they have hands-on experience, and when they can interact with others.

ask yourself

What are your preferred ways to learn about leadership? Why?

How do you play in your leadership development?

Read books, newspapers, journals, whatever you can find. What do others say about leadership? How much of what you read applies to your own leadership interests? Don't forget to read fiction. Fiction provides a wealth of opportunities to apply your leadership knowledge to the characters you encounter. Include opportunities to write about, reflect on, and share what you have read. The discussion will spark further ideas and insights into what you have read, leading to deeper levels of understanding.

Think of a time when you learned something new or changed your mind about something you always thought to be true.

What previous learning have you assimilated? What accommodations of your previous learning have you done to reconstruct new learning?

How do you recognize when a child or another adult is assimilating or accommodating new information?

LIFE EXPERIENCES

Your life experiences are an integral part of your leadership development. Characteristics such as age, race, physical ability, culture, socioeconomic level, educational preparedness, national origin, work experience, career aspirations, and a variety of other factors will have an effect on your life experiences. Your life experiences will, in turn, have an effect on your leadership development because leadership skill, ability, and potential look different in different cultures or subgroups. Try to understand and appreciate both those who view reality from a different perspective and your own individual role and sense of belonging in a multicultural society.

Having lived many years, we each bring a lot of complex personal history to leadership situations. This history includes childhood, cultural, and developmental experiences; knowledge; skills; learning styles; and values, beliefs, and perceptions about ourselves and those with whom we interact. In any leadership situation, there are many people who have not really thought about or examined the impact or the reality of these factors in their lives. There are also those who have a strong sense of who they are and what they can do because they have reflected on these factors. Make sure you are part of the second group. Be sure to set aside time to reflect on who you are and what you think and why.

Your personal leadership development as a teacher and a leader will be affected by how much you have examined and integrated your experiences, values, and beliefs regarding racism, sexism, classism, homophobia, morality, the distribution of resources, and a host of other social, cultural, and political factors that make up the fabric of your world.

For example, those who value distinct and separate roles and responsibilities for men and women may view the process of and purpose for leadership very differently than will those who prefer to blur the lines between gender roles. Those who are used to seeing only European Americans in leadership positions may not be familiar with how leadership looks and sounds when it comes from another culture. Those who believe that most leaders have or should have access to lots of money may think that effective leadership is not readily available in poorer communities. When you have examined your beliefs, values, and experiences, you will be able to think more intentionally about what leadership means to you.

ask yourself

Who are you? How do you describe yourself? Make a list of the key life experiences that have made the biggest impact on how you describe yourself.

Why is each so meaningful to you?

How has each influenced your view of yourself as a leader?

The same systems (such as family, school, culture, community, social services, state and federal government agencies, the media, and larger societal trends) that affect your human development will affect your leadership development. How have these different systems affected your leadership development?

MOTIVATION

Leaders must also possess skills in motivating others. In leadership, you will need to study what motivates you and what motivates those affected by your leadership. Motivation is the incentive to do, change, or accomplish something. There are two kinds of motivation: *intrinsic* (because you want to) and *extrinsic* (because someone or something makes you). Intrinsic motivation is the most powerful and the most lasting because it is linked to your own interests, passions, needs, and desires. Connecting your own interests, passions, needs, and desires to those of others will produce meaningful results and awesome accomplishments. We need to refocus on the deep longings we have for community, dignity, meaning, and love in our professional lives. In general, people are motivated by creative groups and organizations, those that focus on *what* is right as opposed to *who* is right.

When we are motivated by something outside of ourselves (such as money, reward, praise, punishment), it is fleeting because, as we all know, once the motivation is removed, there is little incentive to continue. Sometimes, of course, it is necessary to apply this kind of outside motivation for a period of time with the expectation that inside motivation will take over. We all expect that at some point, the child being made to share a toy (through reward of a treat or threat of a timeout) will develop the inside motivation to share because it is a caring thing to do. In developing your leadership skill and ability, you need a clear understanding of when you are motivated internally and when you are motivated by something external like a reward or fear of a punishment.

ask yourself

What excites you? What makes you angry? What compels you to devote time, energy, and other resources in order to achieve a goal? Focusing on your interests and passions through questions like these can assist you in finding your leadership niche.

What are the interests and passions of your coworkers? What energizes them? Are they aware of their own interests and passions? How can you assist them in the same way that you would like to be assisted by others?

SELF-REFLECTION

Reflection seems like such a simple matter that we sometimes forget how critical it is to leading, teaching, learning, and social change. In its simplest form, to reflect is to take a look at yourself and what you are doing—like looking in the mirror. The power of reflection comes when you do more than just glance at what you see. In a leadership situation, the reflection on your experience, not the experience itself, increases leadership skill and ability.

The answers to your reflections on the "whys" and "why nots" of what you do will take you to the meaningful side of reflection—the place of deep examination and critical analysis. This is an important step in a process for personal and social change that involves theory, reflection, and action. As you read this book, you are affirming, assimilating, and accommodating knowledge. You may come across a piece of knowledge that is very different from what you currently believe to be true or currently understand and you will find ways to assimilate and/or accommodate it. Later, after you've given some thought to what you have read, you may change your previous beliefs as you develop new understandings. A few days later, you might decide to try out a few of these new concepts when a leadership opportunity is presented.

ask yourself

How do you make time for reflection? How do you structure your reflection time? In what ways do you provide opportunities for others (such as colleagues, children, and families) to reflect?

The process of knowing yourself involves remembering, thinking about, and reflecting on past experiences. For all of us, such memories include both good and bad. Unless you are working with a trained professional, such as a therapist, do not spend a lot of time trying to reflect on memories that are very painful and that block your learning. Reflection as a way of developing your leadership ability should be a growing process, not one that inhibits your growth or keeps you from moving forward. This does not mean that you should avoid unhappy or unpleasant memories. Simply ask yourself if the specific memory helps your learning or blocks your learning. Here is an example for using reflection to reconnect with your childhood leadership ability.

exercise

Select an occasion in your childhood when you served in a leadership role. It can be at any point in your childhood. Did you rally the children in your neighborhood to play a new game or hear you tell a story? Were you the captain of the school pep team? Did others seek your guidance or follow your advice? Were you the oldest of several children? Did you organize a neighborhood cleanup or food drive? Did others tend to copy your style of dress? Did you write a poem or story or create a piece of artwork that inspired special feelings in others?

What do you remember about this occasion? Who was there? What was the atmosphere? How did others respond? What was your most favorite aspect of the experience? What was your least favorite aspect?

What messages did others give you about the experience? What did you think about these messages? What influences does this experience have on your leadership strength or ability today? Did you consider yourself a leader then? Why or why not?

Go back and reflect on yesterday, step-by-step. What did you do that worked? What did you do that hindered? How do you know? Was the outcome what you intended or expected? What would you do differently the next time? Are you looking for the right outcome, or is there another possibility?

Reflection on your practice of leadership can take place in a number of ways besides asking yourself questions, just as long as it happens. Discussion with colleagues is a marvelous way to engage in reflection. Mentoring, being mentored, observing, and being observed are also ways to become better at self-evaluation and to increase your leadership strengths. As you experience more practice, more challenges, and more opportunities, reflect on these. Your confidence in yourself and your ability to lead will increase.

ask yourself

Do as children do! Pick something that you did today and ask yourself why. Whatever your answer happens to be, ask yourself why, again . . . and again . . . and again.

Getting to know who you are as a leader will require some intentional thought and dedicated time. A number of questions have been posed to you throughout this book to encourage exploration of who you are and how you came to be you. Put each one of them on an individual slip of paper in a jar. If you reflect on one each day or each week, you will be amazed at how much you will have learned about yourself by the time the jar is empty!

summary

How do you learn to be a leader? You have already started by learning more about yourself and how you began developing leadership skills in your family environment and through the life experiences of parenting and teaching children. You reflected on the influences of individual experiences such as birth order, culture, and learning styles. In chapter 3 you will have an opportunity to learn more about the skills and qualities that make leaders effective. Where do values and vision come from and what role do you play as you make leadership decisions?

How can you increase your cross-cultural competence? How will effective communication and interpersonal skills enhance your leadership? The answers are coming up soon!

story time

Cynthia has decided to open a family child care program. After completing her associate's degree in early childhood education, Cynthia got married and delayed her potential career in order to raise her four children. Being a homemaker was a rewarding experience for Cynthia, but there were times when she thought wistfully of what life would have been like for her had she accepted the position of teaching assistant that she had been offered just after she married.

One of those times was when her oldest son, Miguel, was seven and joined the Little League team in town. Cynthia agreed to organize the carpool schedule for eight families. Then there was the time when Dolores was sixteen and decided that her father had "old-fashioned" views about dating. Cynthia found herself caught in the middle, torn between the need to remain the parent and the need to let her daughter grow up. She managed to help Dolores and her father come to an agreement, but it took a while.

Cynthia was quite pleased at the way the children had grown up to become such admirable adults. She and her husband, Joe, had strong values about education and commitment to the community, and although helping the children stay on top of things at school had been a challenge, Dolores was now a doctor in a neighborhood clinic, Miguel was a supervisor at the plant, Tina was a kinder- garten teacher, and Joey was in the last year of his engineering program at the university. Cynthia had more time on her hands than she had experienced in a long time. Joe wouldn't retire for another five years, and the extra money Cynthia could earn by opening a family child care program would come in handy.

Cynthia decided to take a leadership class at the community center and was pleased with the book she was required to use. It was all about developing and transferring leadership skill and ability from one area of life to another area. **Already, Cynthia was finding out more about how she had developed leadership skills through the process of parenting. It was becoming easier and easier for her to describe to Joe her vision of a family child care program and what steps she would need to take to get there.**

more reading

Darder, Antonia. 1991. *Culture and power in the classroom: A critical foundation for bicultural education.* Westport, Conn.: Bergin and Garvey.

Kouzes, James M., and Barry Posner. 1987. *The leadership challenge.* San Francisco: Jossey-Bass Publishers.

McCaleb, Sudia Paloma. 1997. *Building communities of learners: A collaboration among teachers, students, families, and communities.* Mahwah, N.J.: Lawrence Erlbaum Associates.

Nobles, Wade W., Lawford L. Goddard, William E. Cavil, and Pamela Y. George. 1987. *African American families: Issues, insights, and directions.* Oakland: The Black Family Institute.

Trawick-Smith, Jeffrey. 1997. *Early childhood development: A multicultural perspective.* Upper Saddle River, N.J.: Prentice Hall.

CHAPTER 3

Being an Effective Leader

Now that you have examined the leadership skills you already have and where they came from, let's look at some of the factors that make for effective leaders:

- Cross-cultural openness and understanding
- A clear vision and solid values
- Communication, social skills, and interpersonal strengths

The Cultural Context of Leadership

Culture influences leadership. Communication styles, processes for interacting with others, working with conflict, competition/cooperation, and learning/knowing preferences are just a few of the areas strongly influenced by culture, and it's clear in looking at that list that many of those are essential parts of leadership.

All people need to be able to lead and serve effectively in a multicultural environment. The field of early childhood care and education is extremely diverse in terms of the people who work in it and the families we serve. We must each learn how to lead a diverse group of people and learn how to be led by those who differ from us. Your leadership education and development must focus on how your cultural differences affect your perceptions of reality; what it means to serve a diverse group; how leadership is manifested in different cultures; and how to recognize, encourage, and develop leadership ability in yourself.

Becoming an effective leader means understanding how the world makes sense to others as well as understanding how the world makes sense to you. Your ability to do this as a teacher makes your work with children and their families more effective.

The challenge for new leaders is to unlearn old mind-sets and concentrate on the potential and creativity diversity brings.

You know that trying to get a three-year-old to understand that two different-sized containers can hold the same amount of water is futile. To the child, the tall glass holds more water than the shallow dish. The ability to understand the child's perspective as well as our own gives us the opportunity to create bridges for the child between his world and ours. Leadership is similar. Your ability to understand another's perspective allows you to offer solutions that make sense to others as well as you. If you suggest solutions that only make sense to you, you will be telling others that their perceptions are wrong. Leadership is about solutions that take other perspectives into account.

Leadership in a diverse ECE work environment is a mutual process of leaders and followers working toward a goal, learning from each other, and drawing on the strengths they hold collectively as a result of their life experiences. The challenge for new leaders is to unlearn old mind-sets and concentrate on the potential and creativity diversity brings. In some centers and school-age programs, diversity is not a future possibility, but a current reality.

In other programs, there is more diversity than you may think if characteristics such as age, physical ability, sexual orientation, family structure, educational experience, and socioeconomic level are taken into consideration. The combination of these differences creates a dynamic mix of leadership that can be very powerful.

In my previous position as dean of Pacific Oaks College Northwest in Seattle I had the wonderful opportunity to experience the most multicultural, multilingual, multiracial work environment I have ever encountered. There were eighteen of us and we were equally balanced between four cultural groups: African American, Asian American, Latina, and European American. Languages spoken included English (American, Canadian, and Australian), four regional variations of Spanish (Mexican, Chilean, Guatemalan, and Puerto Rican), Mandarin and Cantonese, and Tigrinya (a language of Eritrea in East Africa). As you can see, even within the four cultural groups there was a lot of cultural diversity. We were able to take the leadership strengths and expectations from all of these diverse cultures to create a new kind of leadership that met most of our individual cultural needs and expectations. This gave us an incredible advantage in working with a variety of families, communities, and racial/cultural groups in Seattle. We also learned a great many new leadership skills from each other—such as how to switch leadership approaches based on the specific community we were working with and how to create teams of different racial combinations to address the needs of early childhood organizations serving more than one racial/cultural group. If your work setting currently serves more than one racial or cultural group, you can increase your leadership ability and your effectiveness by being part of a multiracial or multicultural work team.

Think of all the ways in which you are different from those with whom you work. What are the strengths and skills you bring to a leadership situation as a result of those differences?

In what ways are those with whom you work different from you? What are the strengths and skills they bring to a leadership situation?

WHAT IS DIVERSITY?

Cultural diversity, pluralism, and multiculturalism include all the qualities that make people individuals. They include, but are not limited to, culture, race, color, ethnicity, gender, age, national origin, physical ability, religion, socioeconomic levels, language, sexual orientation, politics, organizational philosophy, intelligence, occupational skills, and attitudes.

Diversity and difference are important concepts in leadership. No two leadership situations will be exactly the same, no one solution will address every leadership need, and two people (or three or four) can "read" the same leadership situation quite differently and come up with two very different yet equally effective ways to proceed. Your leadership task is to notice, appreciate, and take advantage of the diversity and difference each adult brings to the leadership process. Children notice differences among people. It's their job to sort and classify, to notice racial, ethnic, gender, religious, and physical differences (among others). You can add to your leadership ability by beginning to notice differences the way children do. The more you are able to take advantage of cultural differences in leadership, the better chance you'll have of providing leadership that meets the needs of a diverse group of coworkers or a diverse group of children and families.

Because of your knowledge of child development, you understand that there is a lot of variation in patterns of physical development and activity. Not all children do exactly the same thing, in exactly the same way, at exactly the same time. The same is true of leadership. No two leaders will do exactly the same thing, in exactly the same way, under the exact same circumstances. Your work with teachers from other cultures provides lots of opportunities to pay attention to how they respond differently to a leadership opportunity.

There are usually very good reasons for the unique behavior, communication style, expectations, and values of a culture or community. Cultural differences are not the same as developmental deficits, and it is critical for early childhood professionals to understand this and see how the distinction affects their leadership strengths and abilities. A child who is quiet and observant is not less engaged than his outgoing, talkative counterpart. A leader who is low-key and deliberate is not less effective at achieving goals than her charismatic, quick-footed counterpart.

Cultures and communities have strong notions of what is important for their members to know, value, believe, and do. For example, we all learn to communicate with other people. Culture and community influence whether the communication is mostly verbal with very little body movement or eye contact, is all body movement (as in American Sign Language), or is some combination of the two. Culture and community dictate which movements, styles, tones, and expressions are acceptable and which ones are not. Culture and community teach us which of these will feel comfortable and which ones will cause us to feel uncomfortable. In your interactions with others (both co-teachers and the families you serve) you will encounter a variety of communication styles. To be an effective leader and to serve different families effectively, you will need to increase your comfort with and tolerance for many ways of communicating and interacting. The work you do with children every day and the regular interactions you have with their families provide multiple opportunities to practice.

How you lead and how you respond to leadership situations will play a big part in your leadership development. Culture and community determine how we evaluate or define certain behaviors and how much patience and tolerance we have for certain kinds of environments. For example, what some cultures or communities define as "verve" or "vibrancy" may be interpreted by other cultures or communities as "hyperactivity" or "overstimulation." The culture or community in which you grew up will influence your levels of patience with and tolerance for different activities or behaviors. If you grew up in a culture or community where children and adults were relatively still, you might have less patience with the activity and volume levels of a more demonstrative culture. Your work with other teachers, with children, and with their families will be more effective and satisfying when you increase your comfort level with a variety of communication and interaction patterns.

> To be an effective leader and to serve different families effectively, you will need to increase your comfort with and tolerance for many ways of communicating and interacting.

For example, think of a situation where another person disagreed with you or had a different goal or result in mind. Your initial reaction to such a situation is probably based on what you were taught within your culture or community. Did you continue to explain your position? Did you walk away? Did you listen carefully to what the other person was saying? Did you defend your position? Did you give in? What did you learn about the other person? What did that person learn about you?

The amount of competition and cooperation valued in your culture also influences your leadership style. This is even evident in something as simple as the types of games you played as a child. Some cultures value a high degree of competition. In these cultures, childhood games may focus on individual achievement. "Rugged individualism" and determining "the winner" are important values here. Other cultures value a high degree of collaboration and cooperation. Childhood games in such cultures may be less competitive and more collective. In this case, "all for one and one for all" is an important value. You can increase both your leadership ability and your teaching ability by helping your early childhood setting become an environment where competition and cooperation can exist as equal values. Providing "space" for different perspectives and ways of being in the world will give each of your coworkers and the children an opportunity to show what they're good at as well as an opportunity to learn another skill at the same time.

Understanding the cultural contexts of leadership includes understanding how different ways of learning and knowing may be emphasized or valued in different cultures. By understanding several ways in which people prefer to learn, you can begin to transfer that knowledge to your understanding of how, in a leadership situation, people may prefer to learn. For example, African and African American cultures often place a high value on social understanding and the ability to "read" and "write" through body language, facial expressions, style, mannerisms, and tone. In a leadership environment that emphasizes this type of intelligence, you will find more discussion, dialogue, oratory, and dramatic expression. A leadership environment that emphasized movement would include more physical activity such as dance, sport, drama, and use of movement. A leadership environment in ECE should provide opportunities for both adults and children to learn in the ways they like most. You can enact small changes that make big differences to others—changes such as adding opportunities for small group discussions at meetings or having everyone take a walk around the block during a meeting break. Additions such as these indicate to others that you understand that they will learn better (and you will lead better) when a variety of needs are met.

Diversity will always be a part of our lives and experiences. The more you learn about diversity, the more you will understand the benefits to be gained from it. Should you find yourself in a situation where there appears to be little or no diversity, begin asking others what they think about various ideas or directions. Offer a different perspective and see where it leads. Don't allow yourself or your group to fall into the trap of thinking that everyone feels the same way about something or that everyone would make the same choices or decisions. A good leader creates time and opportunity for new and different perspectives, for new and different solutions in leadership situations.

ask yourself

How does your understanding of diversity and your ability to benefit from it affect the work you do with children?

How has your leadership development been influenced by biology, race, psychology, gender, culture, physiology, and all the other exciting, interesting things that happen to us along the road of life?

What differences do you notice in communications styles? In expectations? In the amount of time spent reaching a decision?

Are you the outgoing, talkative, quick-footed type of leader or the observant, low-key, deliberate type of leader? Name three advantages of your preferred leadership type, as well as three advantages of the type you did not select.

Values and Vision

Learning about leadership requires you to think about both values (those beliefs, principles, and ideals that influence both leaders and followers) and vision (perceiving and conceiving of a better place, situation, or circumstance in the future). Your vision is *what* you see as a better future for children, for your place of work, or even for the ECE profession as a whole. Your values are the guidelines that determine *how* you will achieve that vision, what steps or actions you will take. Values and vision are the twin pillars of effective leadership, and both are affected by culture. In a leadership situation, values and vision become a combination of who you are and what you do.

VALUES

Values are the principles and beliefs you hold about what is important and how things are done. They shape how you treat people, the choices you make, and how you see life in general. Your personal values develop in a variety of ways over a lifetime. All human beings have values. Those values may vary according to individual characteristics and circumstances, but most groups of people have some values they hold in common. Knowing what some of those common values are will help you find common ground with coworkers and others, even when you are not always in agreement over a particular issue.

> Values and vision are the twin pillars of effective leadership, and both are affected by culture.

As with descriptions and definitions of leaders and leadership, there is much variety regarding the most important values for leaders and the most important values in the leadership process.

Below are some of the values found in great leaders and in great leadership throughout time and across many cultures and continents.

- Purpose
  (a sense of importance)

- Truth

- Justice

- Empathy

- Empowerment, distributing power among others

- Harmony with others

- Power with, not power over others

- Just words, and actions that match

- Sharing leadership with others

- Discipline

- Caring

- Understanding

- Awareness

- Celebration

- Imagination

- Perception

- Listening

- Openness

- Honesty

- Quality control

- Acceptance

- Fairness

ask yourself

Make a list of your most important values. Where did your values come from? How did they develop? Describe a leadership situation in which you were involved and explain what role each of these values played. Was the situation positive or negative? Why?

How do your three most important values affect how you teach children and the kind of environments you create for them?

SHARED VALUES

A new perspective on values has emerged in recent years, focusing on the leader's relationship with followers. More and more, the literature on leadership is looking at the concept of *shared values* rather than solely focusing on the leader's values. Shared values are the beliefs and ideals that are held in common by the individual and the group. Shared values are the means by which a group of people will achieve their goals and their mission. For leaders, sharing values means that no one person's values take priority, not even the leader's. The workplace will reflect primarily the top two or three values that all of you agree to.

Values such as openness, caring, empowerment, listening, understanding, acceptance, and empathy are indicative of leaders who work in harmony with the needs and desires of other group members. Shared values change groups and organizations by

- Fostering strong feelings of personal effectiveness

- Promoting high levels of group loyalty

- Facilitating consensus about key group goals and stakeholders

- Encouraging ethical behavior

- Promoting strong agreements about working hard and caring

- Reducing levels of job stress and tension

The idea of shared values encourages us to respond positively to one another even when we do not always agree. You and another teacher may disagree on how much the children should be allowed to play with their food during lunch, but if you both share the value of children having nutritious food and keeping meal time a pleasant experience, the two of you may decide to reach an agreement by alternating fun foods with opportunities to teach the children a variety of table manners. Sharing values between leaders and followers enhances two-way communication and facilitates a stronger community and a commitment to the welfare of that community.

ask yourself

What values do you share with your coworkers? What specific shared goals can you accomplish by focusing on these shared values?

Having shared values does not mean, however, that there is only one set of values. Pluralism and diversity are indispensable if we want true commitment to the common good of society. Shared values are a fundamental part of leadership in many cultures and countries on every continent. Without some shared values we will have a difficult time holding a group together during times of struggle, challenge, or disagreement. Without some differing values we will have trouble coming up with innovative solutions, or looking at problems from several different angles.

For example, if you run a family child care program that serves children from more than one religious background, you and the parents may not always agree on what daily activities are appropriate for the children. However, if all the adults can agree that the children should feel good about themselves and should have experiences that teach them about their connectedness to others and how to treat each other with respect, you will all be more willing to continue working through the specifics of daily activities for the sake of holding the community together.

VISION

Vision is another important aspect of leadership. Visions are idealistic, distinctive, and unique, and differ from the current state of affairs. "Creating a vision," "the visible future," and "envisioning the future," are all phrases that refer to your ability to think long-term and imagine what lies ahead or what could lie ahead. When you have a vision, you are able to see the bigger picture, and to imagine a better set of circumstances. A strong vision provides a focus for group members and encourages cooperation.

A good vision has six attributes:

1. Future orientation
2. Image
3. Ideal
4. Uniqueness
5. A collective nature
6. Relevancy to those involved

Looking to the future

A sound vision must be future-oriented. The length of time is not as important as the fact that a vision represents a destination or goal to be reached. A family child care provider starts children working on a collective mural that will be four days in the making. A preschool teacher may spend a month preparing a peace-and-justice classroom management plan and not see the impact on children until the end of the year. A neighborhood group may spend three years implementing their vision of a school-age program that meets the needs of their community. A family may envision a new early learning center

Sharing values between leaders and followers enhances two-way communication and facilitates a stronger community and a commitment to the welfare of that community.

that will take a decade to reach its peak. The common thread in all these situations is the notion of future orientation, a vision of something that does not yet exist.

Having a clear image

Image is the second important attribute of a good vision. Good leaders are like good coaches. All coaches, basically, do the same things, but the good ones know what they want and can see how to get there. The same applies to good leaders. Good leaders not only realize that a better situation is possible, they have an image of what it looks like and how to get there. A good vision contains an image or conceptualization of what is involved in making the vision a reality. Your early childhood program may be considering accreditation as part of its vision for the future. Your role in the leadership process would be to describe your image of an accredited program using words and pictures that show your colleagues what the process would look like, how you would accomplish it, and how the program would be different when you are finished.

ask yourself

What is your vision of your work with children five years from now? How would you go about getting there? What top values would you use to guide you? Why?

Using the vision you described above about your work with children five years from now, explain what that vision looks like. What words would you use to describe the "better place" you have envisioned? What would the children you serve be like? What relationship would you have with coworkers and families?

Dreaming of the ideal

A good vision is idealistic. It must be possible, yet challenging. It may greatly improve on the current state of affairs or create a new state of affairs, but it should not be too easy to achieve. If it is too easy, there is a good possibility that someone else is already doing it. Leaders, at their personal best, engage in "possibility thinking," the "what if . . .?" factor. "What if . . .?" is another way to structure your reflection. Describe what you would do for each "what if . . .?" below. What would each mean for you, for children, for families, for your community or society at large?

- What if you could restructure your work environment?
- What if you had all the money you needed to operate the program you wanted?
- What if you could change the ECE system?
- What if all children grew up to be just like you?
- What if no children grew up to be just like you?

Making it unique

Uniqueness is the fourth attribute of a good vision. Leaders with a good vision strive to be different and take pride in that difference. A unique vision is what sets good leaders apart from everyone else by providing something many want, but few currently provide. This uniqueness creates pride within the group or organization because members take part in creating or producing something new, yet valuable and important. Some of the new specific focus or theme-based centers coming into popularity are examples of unique visions. Centers now specializing in serving children with special needs, centers that are open extra hours, and centers focused on music and the arts are three examples of programs that meet unique needs.

Keeping it relevant

A good vision must be relevant to those involved. Effective leaders know that a good vision is a reflection of group values and involves all group members. A relevant vision is better than the current situation and challenging to achieve, yet linked to the overall strategic direction of the group. You may have a vision of the children you serve becoming bilingual in English and Chinese, to be achieved by having all staff members become bilingual. This would be a challenging vision, yet very meaningful in today's global society. However, if most of the children come from families that speak Vietnamese, the vision would be more relevant to that situation if everyone became bilingual in English and Vietnamese.

ask yourself

How is your vision different from what is happening now? Why is it different?

How does your vision include the vision of your coworkers? Of the children you serve? Of their families and communities? How will you know?

Creating a collective vision

Finally, a good vision must be collective in nature. That is, it must be shared by group members. Although the vision may originate from the leader of the group, it will not become a possibility unless those who must assist in making it happen are as committed as the leader. It may be a wonderful vision to have children exposed to technology by having a computer or two in your classrooms, but it will be the individual teacher in each room who must actually make it happen on a day-to-day basis. The effective leader is able to communicate her vision in a way that attracts and commits others. Below are some strategies for creating a collective vision.

- Use a lot of images and word pictures.

- Appeal to common beliefs.

- Know your audience.

- Include everybody: different cultural groups, all ages and genders, major religions, and so on.

- Say the same things in different ways.

- Spend more time talking about "we" and less talking about "I."

- Be personally convinced that your vision is possible.

These are all ways to communicate your vision to a group of people and win their enthusiasm and commitment. A collective vision changes people's relationship with the program. It is no longer "their" program; it becomes "our" program. Collective visions and values take you from "I" to "we" and from "their" to "our."

ask yourself

How does/will your vision inspire others so they want to join you and be a part of what you want to create? How will you move your group from "I" to "we?"

Vision is always important, whether you are the head of a family, the director of your own family child care or schoolage care program, or the key organizer for a community action group. Any leadership situation in which you find yourself will require you to have a firm idea of and feel for where your group is going and what circumstances and conditions will be like when you get there.

A leader must be able to express herself in words and ways that invite others into the conversation and make them want to stay there and truly listen.

Communication, Social, and Interpersonal Skills

An effective leader works well with other people. Having productive working relationships begins with the open attitude we explored in the section on culture, but it doesn't end there. A leader also must get along well with other people, whether or not he agrees with them, and communicate clearly. What good does it do you, or the area in which you are practicing leadership, if you have a clear vision and strong values, but don't communicate them to others?

COMMUNICATION SKILLS

Leadership involves the ability to communicate and explain what is happening in your environment. The first recognition of a person's leadership potential is often through their verbal skills. ECE employees with strong verbal skills tend to have more organizational skills in the work setting and have the ability to rally coworkers. They do not simply repeat what the director or manager says, but synthesize these views with their own.

An effective communicator

- Is a good listener

- Is listened to by others and sought out for advice

- Asks questions

- Comes up with ideas that are relevant to the issue under discussion

- Speaks well

- Is open to new ideas

- Has a sense of humor

As a leader, you must be able to express yourself in words and ways that invite others into the conversation and make them want to stay there and truly listen. You must also be able to listen to and understand others. You do not have to agree with others, but effective leaders do understand what others are trying to communicate and why they feel as they do about a subject. *Really* listening is a difficult skill to master, but becoming an effective listener is a tremendous step toward good leadership *and* good followership.

- How comfortable are you when communicating with other adults?

- Sometimes, listening to others sparks so many ideas and thoughts that you can't wait to speak. How long can you listen to another person without speaking? How long do you want them to listen to you?

- The next time you are in a casual conversation with someone, practice your listening skills. Make a list of the other person's main points and ask if what you wrote is what they meant to convey.

Have someone whose opinion you value and trust observe you for a couple of days and make notes about your communication with both children and adults.

What do you think of the observation? How will you use the information?

Do you use a different set of communication skills with children than you do with adults? Why do you think this is so?

SOCIAL SKILLS

Social skills are another sign of your leadership potential. They are the way you get along with people and how others get along with you. It seems to be easy for those with strong social skills to get involved with a number of groups both inside and outside of the center. Strong social skills are a necessary part of team building and collaboration, which we will discuss later. You have strong social skills if you

- Like people and make friends easily

- Are honest and build trust easily

- Are warm and outgoing

- Are not afraid to get to know a group of people you don't know very well

- Let others take the credit

- Are flexible

- Have a sense of your own identity

- Are self-directed

- Interact with others in a positive manner

- Have a sense of humor

As you begin to increase your communication and social skills, take some of your cues from the children. As adults, we lose some of our unself-conscious ability to connect with people. When children who don't know each other meet, you'll often hear something such as, "I have one of those at home," or, "What grade are you in?" Adults feel more self-conscious and more awkward. Sometimes, the best we can manage is "Nice weather." Children say things that encourage conversation and dialogue. They want an authentic response. Sometimes, we grownups want to pretend we've had a conversation when we really haven't and really do not want to. We've all been in situations where "How are you?" is really only a rhetorical question!

INTERPERSONAL SKILLS

Strong verbal skills and strong social skills come together to create another important tool in effective leadership—strong interpersonal communication. Interpersonal communication is the ability to

- Sense group attitudes, motives, and feelings, and address these to the satisfaction of group members (such as when a new licensing requirement is under discussion and you can tell that most of the group is opposed, even if they don't all say it out loud)

- Sense the needs of others and respond in a variety of ways, depending on the situation (such as when you are explaining to coworkers a new activity you want to try, and you can tell some need a different kind of explanation)

- Determine what is really happening in an interaction, why people are behaving in certain ways, and what a leader can do about it (such as when you are talking to a parent who isn't fluent in your language and she's nodding her head, but you can tell she may not be understanding everything you say)

- Really care about others, getting to know them well enough to truly understand their viewpoint and communicating effectively so that they truly understand your viewpoint (such as when you intentionally arrange for "getting to know you" time with parents, with no other agenda or business in mind)

These interpersonal skills are essential for effective leadership because they will help you understand the needs of the group you are leading. Use the information to build an effective team. When you use the skills listed, you will spend more time listening to other people and paying attention to how they are responding to you. When you do not use these skills, people may feel that you are not really interested in their participation—what they think and how they feel. Opportunities for team building are lost because team members either have little motivation to implement your ideas or they are unclear on what your ideas actually are!

You can also use these interpersonal communication skills to learn more about how culture influences communication and interaction patterns. As you begin to spend more time with people who are culturally different from you, you will increase your ability to notice and interpret cultural differences in body language and your ability to adjust your own verbal and physical communication patterns. Effective leaders listen carefully when coworkers are trying to communicate in a second language. Effective leaders ask questions and learn more about how different people approach conflicts and disagreements. Your coworkers will notice that you use many different styles and patterns of communication and interaction, and they will feel more like part of a real team. They will be more open with you and will listen more carefully to your perspectives and ways of seeing the world. Good interpersonal skills beget good interpersonal skills!

summary Effective leaders understand that cultural differences and variations influence how we each make sense of the world and how we approach a leadership situation or opportunity. You were able to think more about the values and the vision that define where you want to go and how you intend to get there. Reflection on your communication skills gave you the opportunity to increase and improve your interactions with others. Chapter 4 looks at leadership at every level of the ECE field and how you can increase your collaboration and team-building skills through your work with families and communities.

story time John really wanted to work more collaboratively with his new team-teacher, Mehret. He told her that the two of them should meet weekly to talk about their goals for the children. Mehret liked the idea so John enthusiastically scheduled their meetings and gave her a list of agenda items they could cover. The list included a number of exciting ideas John liked from a workshop he and Mehret had attended that summer and he was looking forward to implementing them.

The meetings seemed to be going well—kind of. Something was not quite right, but John couldn't put his finger on it. Mehret met with him regularly, as scheduled, and she listened politely to all of his ideas and seemed to be quite agreeable. Still, their team teaching did not seem as smooth as it should have been and Mehret often caught him off guard by adding pieces they had not discussed or making unexpected changes. John thought the additions were good; they just caught him off guard.

At a workshop the next month, John told the trainer about his situation. After getting some additional information and listening carefully to how John described his experience, she asked him, "What is Mehret doing and saying during your meetings?" John realized that in his enthusiasm and excitement, he had not paid much attention to what Mehret was doing. She always smiled, but she never said much. John thought about that for a while.

When John got to work the next day, he told Mehret that he realized he hadn't included her in planning their weekly agenda and had, unfortunately, assumed that she liked his ideas because she hadn't said otherwise. Mehret then explained to him that he was always so excited about his own ideas that he never really created enough space in his conversation for her to talk about her own exciting ideas, so she just added them into their curriculum as she could. They agreed that they would take turns planning the meetings and sharing ideas so they could both increase their ability to listen to each other and understand how to take two different viewpoints and combine them in ways that make the curriculum as exciting for the children as it is for the two of them.

more reading

Bolman, Lee G., and Terrence E. Deal. 1997. *Reframing organizations: Artistry, choice, and leadership.* San Francisco: Jossey-Bass Publishers.

Chang, Hedy Nai-Lin, Amy Muckelroy, and Dora Pulido-Tobiassen. 1996. *Looking in, looking out: Redefining child care and early education in a diverse society.* Oakland: California Tomorrow.

Cohen, Allan R., and David L. Bradford. 1991. *Influence without authority.* New York: John Wiley and Sons, Inc.

Gentile, Mary C., ed. 1994. *Differences that work: Organizational excellence through diversity.* Boston: Harvard Business Review Book.

Gonzalez-Mena, Janet. 1993. *Multicultural issues in child care.* Mountain View, Calif.: Mayfield Publishing Company.

Kouzes, James M., and Barry Z. Posner. 1987. *The leadership challenge: How to get extraordinary things done in organizations.* San Francisco: Jossey-Bass Publishers.

Learning Communities Network, Inc. 1997. *Learning from our differences: Color, culture, class.* Cleveland: Learning Communities Network, Inc.

Mallory, Bruce L., and Rebecca S. New, eds. 1994. *Diversity and developmentally appropriate practices: Challenges for early childhood education.* New York: Teachers College Press.

Neugebauer, Bonnie, ed. 1992. *Alike and different: Exploring our humanity with young children.* Washington, D.C.: National Association for the Education of Young Children.

Ramirez, Manuel, III, and Alfredo Castaneda. 1974. *Cultural democracy, bicognitive development, and education.* New York: Academic Press, Inc.

Samovar, Larry A., and Richard E. Porter, eds. 1997. *Intercultural communication: A reader.* Boston: Wadsworth Publishing Company.

Thompson, Becky, and Sangeeta Tyagi, eds. 1996. *Names we call home: Autobiography on racial identity.* New York: Routledge.

Three Rivers, Amoja. 1991. *Cultural etiquette: A guide for the well-intentioned.* Gladstone, Va.: Market Wimmin.

Wheatley, Margaret J. 1994. *Leadership and the new science: Learning about organization from an orderly universe.* San Francisco: Berrett-Koehler Publishers, Inc.

CHAPTER 4

It Takes a Village

I t takes a village to raise a child. We've all heard that. But what does it take to create a village? In a village, every grown-up has a valued, understood role in the education, health, welfare, growth, and development of the children who live there. All of the grown-ups understand this, and all of the children take it for granted. Similarly in the early childhood field in the United States, if you want to influence the lives of children and their families or influence the status and cohesiveness of the profession, it does not matter what level within the field you currently occupy. We can all be advocates and leaders regardless of our roles. We each have a valued and essential role in creating the village that will raise all of our children.

In early childhood care and education, we are still working on creating that village for children—working on truly understanding and valuing each of our roles in raising America's children. Leadership at all levels within an ECE program is a key part of leadership at the local, national, and international levels. This chapter looks at how we each have a role in creating that village for the children, their families, and our profession. Advocacy, storytelling, effective communication, team building, and collaboration are all ways to practice leadership at all levels in our field by increasing our cohesiveness and our connections to each other.

Leadership at Every Level

The strength and enthusiasm of leadership at the middle and lower levels of any group or program creates the strength and enthusiasm at the top.

In order for a program to do its best for children and families, leadership must be present at all levels within every early childhood care and education setting, whether that be a family child care home, a center, a school-age care program, or a preschool. Leader-like actions and qualities must come from every teacher, assistant, aide, and support staff member—every adult. We need to recognize the leadership ability we bring to our own circles of influence—the people we interact with on a regular basis—and begin to make connections between this leadership ability and the ability to influence what happens in our lives and in the lives of children. Leadership does not occur only at the top levels, and it is not always the sole property of the "person in charge." In practice, it is spread throughout all levels, which is essential for a healthy system. Everyone throughout any program or organization must be ready to take leader-like action so each level can function effectively.

Leadership builds on itself. Many of the best leaders in almost any field have come up through the ranks of leadership. Barbara Bowman, president emeritus of the Erikson Institute, began her career as a classroom teacher. Very few people develop leadership

> The strength and enthusiasm of leadership at the middle and lower levels of any group or program creates the strength and enthusiasm at the top.

skills in a brief moment of activity. The leadership talents of some may be well hidden until later years, but with patience, practice, reflection, and the right circumstances, leadership talent will develop and emerge.

Unfortunately, many people imagine that leadership skills such as advocacy, team building, and collaboration belong to professors, lobbyists, and leaders of large professional organizations. Too many people turn leadership into something that they feel they could never attain. This kind of thinking is not only untrue, it seriously inhibits our ability to mobilize the ECE profession and draw on the unique strengths and skills each of us has to offer in the social change process. Any advocacy, team building, or collaboration—any leadership—at any level adds to our power and to our ability to turn things around. The only tools we need are actions and words. The bottom line is that you have to *say* something to or *do* something with someone else, and you have to tell others that you are doing it. Here are some ways to get started.

- Pick an issue or topic that generates strong feelings for you, find out more information about it, link your issue or topic with a larger group of people such as a community organization, decide what you will say or do, and then get going!

- Leadership at all levels means taking action or speaking up wherever you find yourself and wherever you are needed. How do you take action? When do you speak up or speak out?

- Leaders and advocates take action on their good ideas. How do you take action on your good ideas? How long does it usually take you to move from idea to action?

- Arrange times to interview those you consider leaders, at all levels, in a leadership situation. How did they develop their leadership skills and abilities? What challenges have made them who they are today? Who influences them in their lives? What makes them unique? Arrange times for others to observe and interview you. What do they notice about what you do? How do their observations match with your image of yourself as a leader? What can you tell them about your own leadership development?

Team Building

Team building is essential if everyone in an organization is going to be a leader some of the time. Team building in early childhood care and education happens when you create processes, interactions, and activities that help turn a group of people into a team that is effective and efficient at meeting the needs of the children and families you serve as well as your organization as a whole. It is about gathering together all of the people who work in your program (the cook, the driver, the secretary, and the custodian as well as teachers, assistants, and aides) so that everyone has an opportunity to see their roles in working together toward a common goal or vision.

Most ECE programs already have some team-building activities, such as bringing teachers together to think about programming and curriculum or to learn new skills; having a potluck, picnic, or dinner event together; or (in larger programs) having "secret pals" or exchanging gifts during holiday seasons. The best way to build teams is to have every adult who is part of the organization participate in some way. Remember what we said above about every person taking leader-like action at some point so the organization works well? In order for this to happen, everyone in the organization has to be seen as part of the team. For example, custodians contribute to children's learning when they take responsibility for discipline, playground supervision, and modeling appropriate responses to disagreements and conflicts.

Team building is also a way to strengthen your work with your colleagues. It is a way to begin recognizing how each role adds to the leadership the children see in your environment. In my daughter's preschool program, "Miss Fellie," the cook, was just as important in her daily life as "Miss D," her teacher. Every day, my daughter would come home with a story about what Miss Fellie said or did and what she knew about each child's eating preferences. You can start team building by first thinking about who the team is right now and what each person brings to it.

ask yourself

On a sports team, each player has a different role and brings a different strength to the team effort. Make a list of every adult in your program. What is the number one strength or gift each person adds? What would the team and the children be lacking if that person were not there to bring that strength or gift?

What is your relationship with each of these adults? Do you have regular conversations about what each of you wants for the children involved or the families served? If not, ask what each person wants most for the children.

What is each person's relationship with the children? You can learn a lot about who the children think is part of the team by observing their interactions with the other adults in the environment. Ask each adult if they feel like they are part of the team. If yes, ask how. If no, find out why.

Are there support staff in your program? Are they invited to and do they participate in regular program meetings? If they are not part of program meetings, you can suggest that they be invited.

In your role as a leader, you have daily opportunities to talk about your team and to talk with team members. You can be a part of recognizing that everyone is on the team and acknowledging the leadership that takes place on every level in your work setting. You will begin to think differently about your interactions with coworkers, and you will add to the overall team building that takes place in your program.

> Joining forces and resources with families will strengthen your ability to provide children with what they need to reach their full potential.

Collaboration with Families

It is impossible to raise a child in any village that does not involve that child's family! Joining forces and resources with families will strengthen your ability to provide children with what they need to reach their full potential. Family involvement and parent involvement all focus on the important roles of parents and families in the care and education of their children. A number of books have been written on ways to increase and enhance collaboration with parents and families and the importance of having them serve in an ongoing and highly visible capacity in centers, schools, and other early child care settings.

Working with families also will strengthen your leadership ability. Working with families is different from working with colleagues. They play a different role in the lives of their children than you do, and they have different kinds of concerns about their well-being. Of course, they also may come from a different background than you do—a different culture, class, language, or any other continuum of diversity. Learning to balance all these things while you uncover your shared values and your shared vision for the children is the essence of leadership.

The strongest form of collaboration with families is, of course, making sure they have equal voice and equal say in the decision-making process. And this collaboration must be more than just a legal formality or a token gesture. Parents want to feel accepted and encouraged to participate in meetings and activities. Few parents become involved if meetings and activities focus on parents' shortcomings or assume that parents cannot be experts on their own children's strengths and challenges. When parents have equal participation with the early childhood professionals who care for and teach their children, their self-esteem increases, and they enjoy the opportunity to participate as members of a productive and satisfying group. You will also have a stronger, more meaningful relationship with parents and families if they feel they are working with you on behalf of the children.

ask yourself

What is your relationship with the adult family members of the children you serve? Do you have regular conversations with each of them about what they want for the children or the families served? If not, ask each person what he wants most for the children.

GETTING TO KNOW FAMILIES

There are a variety of steps you can take to collaborate with parents to strengthen children's abilities and increase the parents' participation in the leadership process. You can begin a relationship by simply finding out more about each other. Select a family you have not spent much time with and just focus on getting to know them better as people. What are their interests? Hobbies?

What foods do they like best? These little things are the beginnings for having conversations about bigger things, such as goals for children.

Once you have moved beyond the initial discomfort of speaking with a family you don't know very well, you can ask parents and family members if they have a goal they would like to set for the child for the year—a goal you can work on collaboratively. For example, a couple of parents may want their children to retain their home language. You could label or name a few items in more than one language throughout your program as a way to reinforce home language. Begin by letting parents and other adult family members choose the focus of your collaborating efforts. By "letting them go first," you are demonstrating that you do want an equal collaboration, that you respect their role as their children's first teachers, and that the collaboration will be beneficial to them as well. You are giving them some control—an essential component of facilitative leadership.

Getting to know more about the community your program serves is another way to practice leadership at all levels.

As you increase your collaboration with families, they will begin to increase their relationship with you and they will be more open to collaborating with you on a goal that you select— for example, parental/family support in helping a young child use words to express her feelings. It will become increasingly easier for you to form a team with them and work together for the best interest of each child. You will be able to join your forces and resources, recognizing that each of you holds important information about who the child is and what the child needs. The kind of collaboration you learn by working with parents and families will transfer to other areas of your life and to other areas within the profession as well.

GETTING TO KNOW THE SURROUNDING COMMUNITY

You can increase your leadership skills by extending your collaboration with families to include the surrounding community. You don't have to be the head of your program to begin collaborating with the surrounding community and finding out more about it. Getting to know more about the community your program serves is another way to practice leadership at all levels. For all children to be successful we must create new relationships between the children, teachers, parents, and the community—create the village. The first step is to find out more about the community you serve and the relationship you and your program have with the community.

ask yourself

Find out what neighborhoods and communities your program serves. Where do the children live? Do community kids attend your program? Do you know why or why not?

What elementary schools are in the community? Do the children you serve attend more than one? Get to know the kindergarten and first-grade teachers. Invite them to visit your classroom or home program; then, visit theirs. In June, have a potluck with parents of children you serve and invite the kindergarten and first-grade teachers who will have the children next year.

Study the community's history. If the families you serve live in the community where your program is, ask them about the community's history. Has it changed over the years? Is the population growing older or younger? What do you think this means for your program?

ask yourself

How many community organizations are in the neighborhood you serve? Make a list of them and then introduce yourself. Let them know you teach children in the community and get some information on each organization's mission and services.

Check out organizations such as The Urban League and The Boys' and Girls' Club of America. What do they do? Ask your coworkers if there are ways you can work together.

Does your program have an advisory group or board of directors? If not, use the information you've gathered from the community to make suggestions for a new advisory group or board of directors. Be sure that the members are also involved with some of the community groups and organizations.

Doing all of the activities noted above will increase your collaboration skills, make you more knowledgeable about the community you work in, and enhance your role as a member of your work team. And, of course, you will be increasing your leadership ability at the same time.

Advocacy

Leadership in advocacy involves building bridges between the early childhood care and education settings and the communities we serve. All of the issues we face go beyond our work and into the homes and the communities of the children. By finding the links between professional, home, and community issues, we can identify starting points for advocacy. Advocates share their knowledge with others, going beyond good intentions and acting on what they know. Here are some ways to stretch your leadership wings in the area of advocacy:

- Start a parent-teacher association (PTA) for your program if one has not been established.

- Find out where various candidates stand on issues involving children, and vote responsibly.

- Tell parents, friends, and neighbors how you intend to vote and why.

- Pick two or three highlights from a report on the connection between wages and program quality in early care and education, and share them with every adult you meet.

- Find out if the butcher, the baker, and the candlestick maker in your community have children or grandchildren or nieces and nephews. Strike up a conversation about the children they care for and how they are affected by public policy.

- Speak at a conference on how you are developing your leadership and advocacy roles within the field.

- If you are not comfortable presenting at a conference, make arrangements to host an informal conversation on a hot topic at your table during lunch.

- Contact elementary schools and community organizations. Find out what issues you have in common.

- Always be prepared to explain what you do with children and why.

- Support your colleagues in getting more training and education, and support accreditation for your workplace.

- If you are not ready to give testimony at a public hearing, go support someone who is.

- Maybe you are already an actively engaged advocate. Mentor someone else to become an advocate!

Leadership in creating a village means finding the "yes" and the "how" in advocacy, not focusing on the "why I can't." Opportunities for advocacy, like opportunities for all leadership, are presented to us many times throughout the day. Always ask yourself what you can do right now to turn the current situation into an opportunity to speak up or take action on behalf of children, families, and our profession.

Leadership requires the ability to articulate your program's mission, goals, and purpose in ways that others can understand. Your best voice may come from telling stories. In every village there is a storyteller, a person who explains the past, interprets the present, and predicts the future, all through stories. When you tell a story, you bring bits of information to life. Storytelling is certainly no stranger to most ECE teachers!

ask yourself

In what ways do you talk about child development theory to parents and others in the community? What do you say about what you do and how you influence children's growth and development?

What stories can you tell in your own little circle of influence that can spread out to larger and larger audiences?

Have you told the parents a story about how pretend and symbolic play create the foundation for future reading skills? This would be an excellent way to advocate for developmentally appropriate activities for children.

Listen to the stories told in your work environment. What do they tell you? What do you think they mean? When you retell the stories, how do you explain what they mean?

Always ask yourself what you can do right now to turn the current situation into an opportunity to speak up or take action on behalf of children, families, and our profession.

There are so many stories we can share with so many people in so many places. And, don't be apologetic in your telling of a good story. Early childhood educators must become more courageous in standing up for ourselves. The stories we are telling are true and we hold the key to how the story eventually ends. We know that things like higher wages, funding for training, support services for families, and child-friendly legislation all increase the quality of what we do and we should not apologize for that. Leadership as an advocate requires our strong voices. Children require our strong voices because no matter how small you think your voice is, it is bigger and stronger and louder than most children's voices.

summary In helping to create the village, you can use advocacy, storytelling, effective communication, team building, and collaboration with families and communities. Many of these techniques are already familiar to you from the work you do with children, other staff members, and families every day. These activities provide abundant opportunities for everyone at every level of early childhood care and education to lead the way toward better programs, more effective organizations, and a brighter future for the children in our country. Whatever your position in your program, you are a leader in creating the village that can care for all children.

In chapter 5, you will have the opportunity to take a closer look at empowerment, followership, and advocacy. You will think about the kinds of environments that lead to empowerment and your role in creating them. In the section on followership, you will look at the other side of leadership—the strengths, skills, and responsibilities of followers. Then, you will bring empowerment and followership together and take another look at advocacy and its role in changing the ECE profession.

story time

Wei is the director of the after-school program in the community center. Most of the children who participate in the program are East African. For some time now, Wei has been thinking about the fact that the after-school program staff have very few relationships with the East African community and even less knowledge about the history, needs, assets, and resources of the community. The few times she has attempted to have the parents and staff gather informally, she noticed that every single conversation she overheard was based on the familiar roles of the staff and parent discussing the child in the context of the program.

Wei had recently read that when people have an opportunity to interact regularly in situations that take them out of their familiar roles, they begin to discover other shared interests and values and have more authentic conversations about more and more topics. A first step for Wei is to provide an opportunity for the staff to see the children outside of the program. One of the parents tells her about a community festival in which the children will perform a short skit and participate in a parade. Wei decides to work with the children to create invitations to the festival to give to the staff. Creating more complex relationships between the staff and the East African community will take some time, but Wei is excited. She has just received a copy of Participatory Action Research Project Report from the East African Child Care Task Force and many of the action items for the community blend well with the program's mission and goals. Wei knows that attending the festival is just the beginning of an influential collaborative community partnership.

more reading

Bruner, Charles, Karen Bell, Claire Brindis, Hedy Chang, and William Scarbrough. 1993. *Charting a course: Assessing a community's strengths and needs.* Des Moines: National Center for Service Integration.

Etzioni, Amitai. 1991. *A responsive society: Collected essays on guiding deliberate social change.* San Francisco: Jossey-Bass Publishers.

Ghiselin, Bernie. 1987. *Leadership development: The need and response. Community leadership development: Present and future.* Publication no. 50. Report by the National Extension Task Force for Community Leadership. ERIC, ED 288665.

————. 1990. *Forging consensus: Building a dialogue among diverse leaders.* Special Report. Greensboro, N.C.: Center for Creative Leadership.

Kahn, Si. 1991. *Organizing: A guide for grassroots leaders.* Washington, D.C.: National Association of Social Workers.

Kaner, Sam. 1996. *Facilitator's guide to participatory decision making.* Gabriola Island, British Columbia: New Society Publishers.

Mattessich, Paul W., and Barbara R. Monsey. 1992. *Collaboration: What makes it work.* St. Paul: Amherst H. Wilder Foundation.

McCaleb, Sudia Paloma. 1997. *Building communities of learners: A collaboration among teachers, students, families, and communities.* Mahwah, N.J.: Lawrence Erlbaum Associates.

Zander, Alvin. 1990. *Effective social action by community groups.* San Francisco: Jossey-Bass Publishers.

CHAPTER 5

Empowerment, Followership, and Advocacy

In this chapter, you will have an opportunity to think more about what empowerment, followership, and advocacy mean for you as a leader in early childhood care and education. Empowerment is feeling, believing, and behaving as if you have power (in the sense of autonomy, authority, or control) over significant aspects of your life and work. Followership involves examining and reflecting on your responsibilities and influence as a follower and how these affect the leadership process and environment. Understanding empowerment helps you find and use your words and actions in the leadership process. Understanding followership helps you think about the kind of leader and the kind of leadership you choose to support.

In chapter 4, you looked at advocacy as a way to build bridges between our early childhood care and education settings and the communities we serve. In this chapter, advocacy will be discussed from a different perspective: one of speaking and acting from a place of empowerment and a sense of the responsibility of followership. Understanding advocacy will help you combine your newly found internal empowerment with your careful selection of leaders and leadership in order to have more influence in the local and national decisions that impact the ECE profession.

Empowerment

Many people today talk about being empowered, but what, exactly, does that mean? For most people, it means that we want to have more participation and more influence in what happens in our lives and in our workplace. We also want work environments that not only support our participation and influence in making decisions and setting goals, but also appreciate and expect our involvement.

Empowerment is the process of speaking up, speaking out, advocating, and taking action on your own behalf.

Empowerment is the process of speaking up, speaking out, advocating, and taking action on your own behalf. Empowerment is vital to the field of early childhood education because it is becoming more and more important that the general public hear from ECE teachers themselves about the critical role they have in preparing the next generation and about what can be done to increase the quality of the care and education children receive. This is especially important for women, who tend to be socialized to respond and adapt to change led by others, rather than to become actively involved in the change process itself. As a teacher you can begin studying, practicing, and reflecting on empowerment right in your own work environment with your coworkers and the parents and families of the children you serve.

In the dictionary, empowerment is defined as the act of someone *giving* power or authority to someone else. However, if someone "gives" someone else power or authority, that implies that they can also take it away again. For this reason, the best and strongest form of empowerment comes from inside a person (self-empowerment). It is much more difficult for someone to take away the power you find within yourself. Of course, this does not mean that leaders do not have a role in the empowerment process. Leaders create, support, and maintain work environments, processes, and policies that allow others to have some say, some control over what happens (supported empowerment).

Empowerment can seem a lot like participative management, resource or information sharing, delegation of responsibility, or enabling. Participative management, by itself, is not the same as empowerment. Participative management is simply asking people (or allowing them) to participate in the management process. Sharing resources or information is also confused with empowerment. Sharing resources or information without sharing power is not going to result in people feeling, believing, and behaving as if they have control or influence over what happens at work. Delegating responsibility without sharing authority is simply passing on work to another person, but keeping all the power to yourself. Empowerment is also not about enabling. You enable a person when you support an environment and provide people with opportunities to stay *exactly the same way they are now.* For example, suppose you have a coworker who is hesitant to voice her opinion. You would be enabling her to stay exactly as she is now if your solution is to voice her opinion for her. You are supporting her empowerment when you provide opportunities and space in conversations for her to talk and when you encourage others to listen to her.

SELF-EMPOWERMENT

Self-empowerment takes place when you decide to do something or say something in order to change a situation. You may be a person who has little trouble doing this or you may be someone who has never really done anything like this before. Let's say you have a colleague who always seems to notice when the boys are misbehaving, but not when the girls are. You really wish she would treat the children more equitably. Being empowered means you say something to her—even if you think her feelings might be hurt or she might get mad at you, even if you tend to be shy, even though you are not her supervisor. Perhaps nobody told you that it was okay for you to talk to her, or that you were expected to bring up troublesome issues with your coworker. Nobody gave you the power or the authority to do that. You simply recognized that you had the power to address a difficult situation, and you did. That is self-empowerment. (It's also leadership!)

SUPPORTED EMPOWERMENT

Supported empowerment takes place when you and all of your colleagues work together intentionally to make sure that everyone has an opportunity to state what they want to have happen and that everyone's perspective is not only valued, but heard and responded to. Remember the coworker we discussed above who seems hesitant to voice her opinion. If speaking for her would be enabling, how can you support her empowerment to speak for herself? Supported empowerment means that you pay attention to her hesitation to speak up. You make space in conversations by asking her what she thinks. You encourage others to ask her opinion. You make sure you listen carefully to what she has to say, even if you do not agree.

> True empowerment is being intentional about making sure that the work environment encourages and supports the full participation of all members.

Or consider the example of the coworker who is treating boys and girls differently. Perhaps you have a group agreement that teachers in your program will talk to one another about difficult issues and will raise concerns they have about how the program is working. Perhaps you have a director who specifically asked you how your working relationship was going. When you tentatively voiced your concern about how boys and girls are treated differently, she offered to help you think through how to approach your coworker, or to debrief with you afterwards, or to mediate if your concern became an open conflict. These are all examples of supported empowerment. You still have the power you always had to talk to your coworker, but the system and the people around you are supporting you to use that power. (And yes, you are still a leader in this situation!)

AN EMPOWERING WORKPLACE

True empowerment is being intentional about making sure that the work environment encourages and supports the full participation of all members. True empowerment is not just to be able to say that everyone participated, that you shared information or resources, that you delegated responsibility, or that you helped someone. You want empowerment because of the unique strengths and potential each person brings to the work experience. You want empowerment because you want each person to develop into a strong and capable person. You want empowerment because you want to hear what others think, believe, and want. You want empowerment because the change that comes from shared power and influence lasts longer. True empowerment means you want all of this for yourself, and you will create, support, and maintain an environment that provides it for others.

What does an empowering environment look like? What actions and processes would you see? Below is a list of some things to look for.

- People freely share their opinions and perspectives.

- People openly seek out other opinions and perspectives.

- People really listen to each other, and they listen in order to understand what the other person has to say.

- There is a lot of collaboration and sharing; people do not feel the need to ration their energy or their resources.

- At meetings, there is much lively conversation, and everyone participates.

- Most decisions are made by the whole group, not two or three individuals.

- People willingly participate in decision making because they know their opinions and perspectives matter to the rest of the group.

- Even when a few people do not agree with the decision that is made, they know that they didn't "lose." Their opinions are valued. They are comfortable with the decision-making process even if the decision is not the one they would have made.

- How people feel about things is evident to everyone. There is not a tendency to hide feelings in order to protect oneself.

- Even those who tend to be shy or quiet are seen sharing their opinions and perspectives, and new people join in faster than they would in an un-empowering place.

ask yourself

Describe the ways in which your work environment empowers you. Are there ways in which your work environment seems to take power away?

In what ways do you share resources, information, and authority? In what ways does this empower you or empower others? Why does it empower you or others?

Empowerment does not mean you'll always get your way. There will still be times when things do not turn out the way you want. Being empowered does ensure, however, that you did your best to make sure your needs and expectations were heard.

Empowerment is leadership that is shared, not the responsibility of a lone individual. It can only happen when each of us learns to collaborate, cooperate, and include all members. This is particularly important when considering collaboration and community leadership. When you have an opportunity to take an active role in how your work is designed and how your work is conducted, you will be more effective.

YOUR ROLE IN SUPPORTING EMPOWERMENT

As a leader in early childhood care and education, you can assist in the empowerment process in two ways. First, you can help create an environment that allows team members some control over their responsibilities and some confidence in their individual ability to create change. Second, you can examine your own feelings of control and self-confidence.

The first step is empowering ourselves. When you are empowered you become a model for others, and they can learn from your example. There are many ways to begin respectfully and firmly increasing the amount of influence and control you have at work.

- Tell others what you are feeling, thinking, sensing.

- Clearly explain what you want, need, expect.

- If an action or behavior conflicts with your personal values, say so.

- When someone speaks to you in an inappropriate manner, explain that you do not like to be treated that way.

■ When you meet someone for the first time and he shortens your name (Debra to Debbie) or changes it (Juana to Jane) correct him.

If you have not had a lot of practice, this process of empowering yourself will not be easy at first, but it can be very rewarding. I have never liked any ethnic jokes, and when I was about twenty years old, I decided that I would not let people tell them in my presence. It was very difficult at first, because those who were older than me tried to ignore my request, and those who were my age or younger would tease me and make fun of me. ("Close your tender ears, Debra! I'm about to tell an ethnic joke!") Sometimes I just left the room, and other times I stood my ground. Twenty-five years later, none of my friends and relatives tells ethnic jokes around me, and I'm no longer teased or ignored. Some of them probably do not tell such jokes at all because I ruined the fun for them, but I felt good about standing my ground, and it worked.

> Empowerment calls for new leaders, creative women and men whoinspire others to go beyond simply carrying out tasks and to move toward collaboration and consensus building.

Empowerment calls for new leaders, creative women and men who inspire others to go beyond simply carrying out tasks and to move toward collaboration and consensus building. Empowering leaders must be compassionate, people-oriented, and sensitive to the needs of diverse groups and individuals. They must be "social architects" who mold and shape the work environment so that it supports and encourages group and individual control and influence. As a teacher in early care and education, you are a social architect already, because everything you do as a leader changes the environment around you.

ask yourself

Describe how empowerment plays a role in your own personal experiences. This can be about how you felt empowered or how you assisted in creating an empowering environment for others.

Followership

With all the discussions regarding leadership, few have conducted the ultimate test of effective leadership: Is anyone following? "Followers" and the concept of "followership" have received increased attention lately in the study of leadership. Many of us may not reach the top levels of leadership in our workplaces or professions, but in order for us to identify who is a good leader, we must be able to fully recognize what makes for effective leadership and be aware of how we have developed those same qualities in the course of our everyday lives. All of us—teachers, assistants, aides, parents, trainers, and directors—must be able to *recognize* a good leader and resolve to *follow* only good leaders.

The word "follower" has negative connotations for some who may think of followers as passive and dependent. The myth of the passive follower fits well with the myth of the leader as the primary mover of history and change. In fact, no one leads all the time. A leader in one context is a follower in another. A good leader in one context is likely to make a good follower in a different context, because the same skills are needed. For this reason, leaders are most effective if followers are strong in their own right.

According to Robert Kelley (1992):

- Leaders only contribute an average of 20 percent to the success of most groups.

- Followers are crucial to the remaining 80 percent of that success.

- Most people, regardless of title or salary, spend more time working as followers than as leaders.

Followership is a very responsible role. Followers take the risk to empower the leader, and it is the followers who must hold the leader accountable. In fact, followers often determine who is acceptable as a leader and if that leader will be effective. Followers show their leaders where to walk, and they validate the words leaders speak on their behalf. In essence, the follower grants leadership to the leader.

ask yourself

What do you look for in a leader? What do you notice in effective leaders?

Followership is a serious responsibility. Choose a circumstance in which you would describe yourself as a follower. Describe the responsibilities you have in this role. As examples, you can focus on your role as an employee, a voter, a daughter or son, a customer, or a client.

Ira Chaleff, the author of *The Courageous Followers: Standing Up To and For Our Leaders*, identifies five dimensions of courageous followership:

1. **The courage to assume responsibility.** Effective and courageous followers understand that part of their role in the leadership process is to be responsible for anyone they allow to lead them, speak for them, and act on their behalf. If you find

yourself following someone who is engaged in activities, actions, or behaviors that conflict with your expectations, needs, and values, you must take responsibility for supporting such a leader and decide what you intend to do about it.

> All of us—teachers, assistants, aides, parents, trainers, and directors—must be able to *recognize* a good leader and resolve to *follow* only good leaders.

2. **The courage to serve.** Effective followers understand the importance of service to others. Just as leaders need to be in the service of followers, courageous followers must be in the service of leaders. When you firmly believe in the vision, direction, and goals of a leader, you must support the leader and the leadership process through your words and your actions. You must engage in activities and behaviors that help contribute to the group's ability to meet its goals or accomplish its mission.

3. **The courage to challenge.** Effective and courageous followers must challenge and push their leaders toward a higher standard. If you notice that your leader is veering from the course set by the group, you have a responsibility to question the change and expect a response. Sometimes it is difficult to say, "I don't think that is what we had in mind," but if you do not, your inaction can be misinterpreted as consent or approval—whether you mean it to or not.

4. **The courage to participate in transformation.** Courageous followers know that change is hard, and they know that leaders cannot transform any workplace alone. Your actions, behaviors, attitudes, and expectations have just as much impact on your workplace as your director's or

supervisor's. Effective followers understand that they are just as responsible as their leaders for how or whether the workplace changes, so they participate actively and intentionally in the change process.

5. **The courage to leave.** Sometimes, there simply is no way to reconcile your values with those of your leader. When this happens, courageous followers leave and seek an environment that more closely matches their values. This is often the hardest thing followers must do, especially if it means being unemployed for any length of time. There are alternatives, such as staying and being an unwilling supporter of something you do not believe in, or adjusting your own values to be more in line with your workplace. It takes courage to decide you must leave.

ask yourself

How would you describe yourself in each of the five dimensions of courageous followership described above? In what ways could you be a more courageous and effective follower?

The choice between leading and following is not an "either/or" situation. Leadership and followership are more like the ends of a continuum. Where we are on that continuum depends on the roles each of us plays and on the groups we are involved with in the various aspects of our lives. All of us have been, or will be, both followers and leaders in the course of our lives. Followers often perform leader-like acts and exhibit the same skills, styles, and abilities as good leaders. This does not necessarily mean that leaders must wait for followers to tell them what they want.

Although followers like being treated with consideration and respect, and although they appreciate opportunities to give input and to be creative, followers also expect leaders to provide clear direction and decisions and to take authority when and where it is needed.

ask yourself

Leadership ▬ ▬ ▬ ▬ ▬ ▬ ▬ Followership

Pick two groups in which you are active. Where would you place yourself on the continuum above for each one? Why? In what ways do you move left or right on the continuum for each group?

The relationship between leaders and followers is one of interdependence. Leaders never have as much control as the myth of the all-powerful leader suggests, and followers are rarely as submissive as the myth of the passive follower suggests. Authority and responsibility for the leadership process belong to both the leader and the follower, and both need to develop new beliefs and expectations for leader and follower roles.

In the leadership process, leaders and followers depend on each other to meet their individual needs. Family child care, centers, and school-age care programs need children and families, politicians need voters, businesses need customers, social service agencies need clients, supervisors need the cooperation of their workers, religious organizations need members. And we, in any of these follower roles, need the organizations we are a part of.

Effective followership is both thoughtful and intentional and must be taken seriously. What we do with our individual or collective power as followers determines what our leaders will do for us. Think about your workplace as an example. Yes, you may need your job as a teacher, and families may need safe, healthy, and educational play and learning environments for their children, but directors, supervisors, and family child care providers need you and the families as well. They need quality teachers and care providers if they want to maintain the quality of their programs. They need children to fill their programs. If either party is unhappy with the goals, values, attitudes, and actions of the other, the working relationship will fail, and someone (such as you, a family, or the person in charge) will begin thinking about other options.

> Effective followership plays a vital role in not only creating your workplace vision, but in carrying out that vision.

Effective followership plays a vital role not only in creating your workplace vision, but in carrying out that vision. Groups and organizations that are on the cutting edge seek out independent, critical thinkers who have the courage to stand up for their ideas and beliefs. Naturally, providing an environment that supports effective followership means that the environment is an empowering one as well. Unempowered people do not display the kind of followership we have just been discussing. Empowerment and followership must go hand in hand if the early childhood field is to take full advantage of the combined potential of its members. If you feel empowered enough to make your expectations and values known to your coworkers, you will feel empowered enough to make them known to your supervisor. If you feel empowered enough to make them known to your supervisor, you will have begun paying closer attention to your supervisor's leadership and how it matches your expectations of a leader. If you are paying attention to your expectations of leaders and leadership, you are taking your responsibility as a follower more seriously. If this is true, you may well be ready to have a bigger voice in a much larger conversation. You may well be ready for an expanded role as an early childhood care and education advocate.

Advocacy

Leadership in advocacy can be a matter of increasing your connections to families and communities as covered in chapter 4. Leadership in advocacy can also be a matter of broadening your circle of influence, gaining the ear of more and more people who make decisions and choices about the early care and education field. In many ways, this will begin to happen naturally as your sense of empowerment and sense of followership grow. You will find yourself connecting with others who share your values, goals, and vision and you will push, encourage, and support each other toward higher levels of action.

Like empowerment, however, advocacy must come from within. Only you can transform yourself into an advocate, because your role as an advocate can only be defined in terms of your actions, those steps you take to improve the lives of the children, their families, and those who work to serve them. It is when all of our individual efforts combine that we begin to experience the difference a village can make in raising a child. There is a saying that you are only one drop in the ocean, only one tree in the forest, but without all those drops there can be no ocean and without all those trees there can be no forest. In advocacy, never assume that someone else will do it and that therefore your little piece of action won't matter. When too many people make this assumption, we never get enough drops of water to make an ocean or enough trees to make a forest.

Most people who have changed the way we and others view our work did not set out to create a societal or national movement. Most of them only set out to stick with some idea, values, or activity that inspired their passion. One example is Maria Montessori, who did not set out to create an internationally known curriculum. She was only interested in accommodating a group of Italian children in need of something new and different in their learning environment. At the same time, she was an advocate for the children.

To be an advocate at this level is to take on a leadership role discussed earlier, that of a spokesperson who carries forth the voices of those who may go unheard. This kind of advocacy is essential to the ECE field as we continue to address recognition, professionalism, quality care and education, adequate resources, and the creation of coordinated programs that serve children and prepare them for kindergarten.

A good advocate is passionate about, committed to, and believes strongly in her goal. A good advocate also knows deep down that it is possible to meet that goal. A good advocate will use many of the same leadership skills and abilities that you have been examining throughout this book:

- Courage

- Good communication and speaking skills

- Planning

- Vision

- Persistence

- Commitment

- Persuasion

- Clearly defined values

Do you have a goal, a vision, or an idea that you just know is not only possible, but is desperately needed? Have you asked others if they feel the same way? Who have you talked to? What have they said? What could be some next steps for you?

In the previous chapter, there is a list of activities you can begin doing as an advocate, building bridges and links with families and communities. Here are some "next steps" to help you see the possibilities for broadening your circle of influence with a few of those activities, in order to have more impact on the local and national decisions that affect early childhood care and education.

- Start a PTA for your program if one has not been established. **Next step:** Arrange for your program's PTA to meet with the local elementary school's PTA.

- Find out where various candidates stand on issues involving children, and vote responsibly. **Next step:** Work on the campaign team of a supportive candidate.

- Tell parents, friends, and neighbors how you intend to vote and why. **Next step:** Ring doorbells for the candidate who supports your favorite ECE initiative.

- If you are not ready to give testimony at a public hearing, support someone who is. **Next step:** Sign up to give testimony.

- Always be prepared to explain what you do with children and why. **Next step:** Make an appointment to do this with your local senator or representative.

summary

In this chapter, you had an opportunity to think about empowerment, followership, and advocacy and what they mean for you as a leader. All three must come from within, and all three require you to think about your own power, control, actions, influence, and choices. When you are an empowered advocate who makes responsible followership choices, you will be taking on a larger leadership role in advancing the goals and objectives of the early childhood education field.

You have now reached the end of this book, but not the end of your journey. In many ways, your journey is just beginning. You have been introduced to many ways of looking at and thinking about leadership and your role in the leadership process. Leadership takes place in a variety of forms and contexts, and on a variety of levels. Continue on your reflective jouney as you think about what leadership means to you and about who you are as a leader. Every time you interact with another person, you have the opportunity to bring leadership to life through interdependence, service, respect for cultural variations, interpersonal communication, empowerment, and advocacy.

Remember that leadership is developmental. Take your time and be patient with your own learning. Take extra care of the leader in you. You can only get better and better. We need your leadership! The children, their families, and the field of early childhood care and education all need what you have to offer. Every lifelong journey begins with a single step. I think you are well on your way!

story time

Veronica was in a tight spot. Her after-school program had just merged with another program, combining the staff and the children into one building. Veronica had been with the program for a year and had enjoyed working with her team. At first, Veronica thought that combining the two programs was a great idea. She knew many of the other staff members and many of the children knew each other because they lived in the same general neighborhood. So why was Veronica uncomfortable?

As the weeks passed, Veronica noticed that the two sets of staff seemed to stay separate and were even beginning to say unkind things about each other. It reminded her of how kids on the playground behave: they were whispering in little groups and hoarding resources. They referred to the children as "my children" and "their children." She thought about saying something, but she had always kept to herself most of the time, and since she had not been with either program as long as some of the others, she wasn't sure it was her place to say anything.

Veronica did not really like the new work environment being created, not for herself and certainly not for the children. She had waited several more weeks for someone to do something or say something, but no one did. She didn't like the way she was being treated by the folks from the other after-school program, and she didn't like the way the staff from her original program wanted her to join them in saying bad things about the others. She certainly didn't like the way the "leaders," who were now codirectors, seemed unable or unwilling to talk about what was going on. Veronica could not see herself coming to work every day and being a part of all this much longer. She started looking for another job.

One day, one of the children came to Veronica and told her that a staff person from the other program always played favorites with her own kids and always sided with them when the two groups of children had disagreements. That moved Veronica right out of her tight spot! It did not matter if her coworkers were really playing favorites or not. What mattered was that the children thought they were. Although Veronica had never been one to speak up or speak out, she knew she could not in good conscience leave without advocating on behalf of these children who were picking up on the unkind behavior the adults were modeling.

Veronica could not, in good conscience, continue to follow the poor leadership that currently existed—but first she needed to let her coworkers and the codirectors know how she felt. The next time she felt pressured to join in disrespectful conversation, she gave a firm "no" and explained that she did not want to be a part of "bad-mouthing" the others. She also spent time seeking out individual members from the other team and trying to break down the communication walls. Finally, Veronica went to the two codirectors and explained to them that there was too much "us" and "them" in their after-school program and that it was unhealthy for the children. Naturally, they both denied that this could really be happening, but they said they would take a look at it.

Veronica did eventually leave, but for the weeks between the time she put her foot down and the time she left, she felt awkward at work. Some people were afraid to talk to her, and others were just plain mad at her for pointing out their bad behavior. It was hard for Veronica, but she felt stronger than ever. She had taken a risk on behalf of herself and the children in the after-school program, and she had stood firm.

more reading

Chaleff, Ira. 1995. *The courageous follower: Standing up to and for our leaders.* San Francisco: Berrett-Koehler.

Darder, Antonia. 1991. *Culture and power in the classroom: A critical foundation for bicultural education.* Westport, Conn.: Bergin and Garvey.

Freire, Paulo. 1986. *Pedagogy of the oppressed.* New York: The Continuum Publishing Corporation.

Guillebeaux, Jack A. 1998. *More is caught than taught: A guide to quality child care.* Montgomery, Ala.: Federation of Child Care Centers of Alabama.

Kelley, Robert. 1992. *The power of followership: How to create leaders people want to follow and followers who lead themselves.* New York: Doubleday.

Index